Mavis
And
I...

"Gerry Pyves has succeeded with this profoundly moving novel in narrating the essence of how mind/body/spirit are all connected, and how professional and intuitive bodywork can be utterly transformational to ordinary people's lives. I read it from start to finish in one evening and found it completely riveting....... Mavis is truly a metaphor for every unique individual alive."
Sandra Goodman, Ph.D. (author of "Nutrition and Cancer" and publisher of "Positive Health Magazine")

"What a pleasure and an opportunity it is, to have an experienced guide walk us through the shadowy territories of conscious touch, and more importantly share the consequences that follow in its wake. The power of an educated touch is potentially the most awesome of therapeutic tools. This book will open your mind to the wonders to be found through conscious touch..."
Don McFarland (author of "Body Secrets" and founder of Body Harmony®)

"I will buy a copy of this book to give to my Mum, so that she can finally understand why I do what I do."
Trudi Schaller (Massage Therapist, Perth)

Mavis and I...

Gerry Pyves

SHI'ZEN PUBLICATIONS

Published by Shi'Zen Publications
PO Box 57, Hebden Bridge, West Yorkshire, HX7 6WW
+44 (0) 1422 843 842

Printed by SwiftPrint, Huddersfield

ISBN 0 9539074 4 9

I dedicate this book to

Geraldine

*So often I look back and see only
one set of footprints in the sand...*

Yours

There is but one temple in this Universe
And that is the human body

We touch heaven
When we lay our hands upon it

Based on an extract from Thomas Carlyle

Acknowledgment

I acknowledge every single client who lay on the table and courageously breathed and released and thereby taught me everything I know about the power of touch and how unique it is for each individual. You wrote this book.

I acknowledge every single student who has trained with me and persisted in both challenging and trusting everything I have shared. You honed my understanding.

I acknowledge Don McFarland whose teachings and book *Body Secrets* opened the door into the magical world of healing touch for me. Your influence permeates every page of this book...

I acknowledge Mariella Severynen for your loving support and your meticulous proofing.

About Massage

Wherever the word Massage is used as either a noun or an adjective I have given it a capital M. I regard Massage as a significant therapy and therefore afford it the same courtesy as other 'capital letter body-therapies' such as Reflexology, Aromatherapy or Osteopathy. Wherever the word Massage is used as a verb, as in *"I massage my friend"*, I have reverted to the more common usage.

It's a *peccadillo* of mine.

About Dialects

In his *"The Adventure of English"*, Melvyn Bragg describes the significance of dialect. He explains how for many, dialect is held on to with pride because it is a clan thing. It has been created by the clan and it carries the raw and confident energy that all groups who are brave and strong enough to stand up against the establishment possess. Dialect is the language of outsiders who will not be overrun. Dialect cocks a snoop at all who abuse power by attempting to subjugate others through 'proper language'.

In short, dialect is the language of those who would be free, in the face of oppression.

Prologue

What follows is the fictional story of Massage and touch for one particular individual.

The truth of the matter is that it is drawn from the reported experiences of hundreds of Massage clients.

And everything in it actually happened...

Chapter One

The connection is made.

In a house several hundred miles away, the phone rings and a woman's voice answers in thick scouse,

"Hello? Mavis here."

Very here.

Very *rock solid* by the sound of it, this Mavis. Very absolute. Someone so certain of herself that being here is a given, an unquestionable so to speak.

"Oh I say, hello Mavis, it's... ah, Grant, here."

Grant the Massage therapist. Grant the incompetent, actually - but don't tell anyone, will you old sport? It's about 9.30 on Saturday morning and I'm standing in a phone booth in the middle of nowhere.

"So... are you, um... well, Mavis?" I ask.

It is pouring with rain and I'm looking out over a very grey Loch somewhere in the far north of Scotland. Loch Broom, I think it's called and it brushed away all the sunshine before we arrived, it did.

"Oh hi Grant! This is a surprise! How are yer? How's the new baby doing - what is he, three months old now?"

This is only my second conversation with Mavis and I should already confess to a degree of envy.

It's this *certainty* of hers.

By contrast, I seem to stutter through every absolute I meet with the distinct feeling that it is really only a question mark in disguise.

"Well, we're all fine thank you, Mavis. Quite fine actually. Baby's a treat. Absolute star. Won't sleep a wink of course, but melts all our hearts every time he smiles at us so we forgive him, don't we?"

"Aw that sounds good. Sounds like yer probably too soft

on him, though" she laughs.

"Well absolutely," I laugh "Soft as marshmallows we are, Mavis..."

I know I am just postponing the moment.

The moment of incompetence

I look out of the grimy phone booth. The rain is blowing great squalls of shadow across the loch surface. Rather beautiful, actually. Well,

Here goes,

"Listen, I am *terribly* sorry to call you on a weekend like this but have you got a minute?"

" 'Course I have, I ain't doing nothing that won't wait. So what can I do for you - hold on - I thought you was away on yer holidays?"

My wife is still asleep in our holiday cottage up the lane; it has been another bad night with baby Petey. I find myself wondering at just how crazy we are. I mean, fancy going on holiday with a three-month old baby and exposing him to the bitter cold of a summer holiday in Scotland!

I look out of the phone booth into the drizzle and watch my ten year old son, Luke, cycling happily back and forth along the deserted road. His six year old sister, Heather, plays bravely on her little green bike; the one with the back wheel supports on it.

The rain and the cold do not bother them, of course.

It is one of those moments I just know I will always remember: standing in a remote phone box beside a pink-hued Scottish road with Luke and Heather playing on their bikes while I am trying to cancel my appointment with Mavis.

The road stretches straight on past us into the far distant hills, now covered in mist.

Deja vue, perhaps? What I do know, is this:

I am cold.

I am exhausted.

"Yes, well Mavis, that's the problem you see. This is a bit of a *mea culpa* call, I'm afraid."

I take a deep breath and continue:

"You see, it's about your appointment on Monday. We've decided to extend our holiday in Scotland we have, Mavis. So I'm really calling to see if we can *postpone*, I'm afraid."

"Aw right, I see..."

Silence.

"Well, that's a shame..." she says.

More silence.

"Still, don't worry about it..." She continues, "These things happen don't they?"

There is another awkward silence.

I'm not sure what to say.

Then Mavis says *stoically*, "So, are yer all having a good time, then?"

"Well we are. Absolutely." I reply, "I mean the plan *was* to return back to base today, but the kids are having such a good time... You know what kids are like with holidays, Mavis, they seem to positively *devour* them, don't they?"

"Tell me about it!" She laughs, hiding her disappointment well. "Good on you, Grant, for taking yer family away like that - sounds great!"

"I am so terribly sorry, Mavis, I mean letting you down like this. No excuses. *Mea culpa*, see?"

"Aw, don't be daft, man! You only got yer kids once and before you blink they'll be asking yer to help with paying the ruddy mortgage an' all!"

"Well absolutely, but I'm awfully sorry... I really am."

Despite her acceptance, I really do dread these calls where I have to cancel. I know just how much importance can be attached to a session.

"Anyroads," she continues, "I was a bit surprised that you was working on a Bank Holiday Monday, anyway..."

Bank Holiday?

Bugger!

How on Earth did you manage to miss that one, Grant?

"Oh dear. So is it really a Bank Holiday on Monday, then? ...this *next* Monday?"

"Yeah! But then maybe not in Scotland," she laughs. "You know what a queer bunch they is up there! I mean the men walks around in ruddy skirts, for starters, don't they?"

Then she adds in her thickest Liverpool brogue, "Nor 'n can they talk proper, neither!"

We both laugh at her self mocking joke.

The thing is, Mavis strikes me as a really *good* person.

I remember reading her letter asking for a Massage appointment. There was something, well, warm about the letter.

Something must have made me prioritise her because I don't normally work on Mondays - Bank Holiday or not.

"Oh dear, I didn't even realise it was a Bank Holiday, Mavis, what an absolute *goon* I am. Listen, I know it's proving jolly hard to get this appointment but do you think it would be possible for us to reschedule? Could you manage that at all, Mavis?"

" 'Course I can."

Then there is another pause. This time I am sure I can hear her smiling as she adds,

"But you won't have yer appointment diary with you... not on yer holidays, surely?"

"Ah... er, no. Well, good point, actually Mavis. Not right here with me, as it happens..."

You really are doing exceptionally well today, old boy Excelling yourself, actually. In the incompetence department, that is

"I tell you what Mavis, do you think I could give you a ring as soon as I get back home, perhaps? Would that be all right with you?"

It's at times like this that I feel I should be doing something else entirely; that I'm not really up to the job of helping others at all. I think there is something intrinsically *conceited* about all us therapists. The very idea that who we are and what we know can help another person is full of a kind of *hubris* of the worst order.

I mean, put your own house in order before trying to help others, Grant.

Hubris

Don't you think?

My own house is a shambles, actually... We don't ever seem to get on top of it.

As I'm talking to Mavis, the sky seems to brighten, hinting at a possible breakthrough from our long lost friend, the sun.

Perhaps we can make that planned trip to the coastal beaches today, after all?

"That's fine, Grant." Mavis says, bringing me back down to Earth. "You enjoy yer holidays and give us a ring when you're back."

"Well that's jolly decent of you, Mavis."

And then, as an afterthought I say,

"Oh, and Mavis?"

"Yeah?" she responds.

"Well. You know... Thank you."

"Aw get on with yer!"

I don't really know why, but as I walk back up the lane with Luke and Heather, I feel lighter and somehow, *absolved*. Isn't it odd how complete strangers can sometimes do that to us - create ease and hope without really doing anything, except be themselves?

I smile again at her joke:

Nor 'n can they talk proper, neither

And then the surreal image of a red-bearded Scotsman holding up his kilt and dancing ever so daintily whilst singing incomprehensible rasping Gaelic floats into my mind...

I smile to myself.

So perhaps this day will go well after all, despite my exhaustion.

I feel my energy begin to lighten.

"Wheeeeeeee!!!!!!!!!" Heather squeals, as I run up behind her and push her little bike at high speed. We race Luke all the way back up to the cottage, screaming and laughing.

Where did I put those buckets and spades?

Chapter two

I leaves several messages on this posh fella's answer phone in Halifax, somewhere in Yorkshire, don't I?

And after about the fourth message he still hasn't replied, has he?

So I writes him a letter to say I wants a session with him - because it helped me shoulder so much when he gave me that treatment on the course, like. And in me letter I tells him as how I can come any day of the week while our Mickey is at the day care centre. So long as it's in the middle of the day and I can get meself back in time for him, like.

And what does I get for all me trouble?

Nothing.

Not a friggin' squeak!

So it's about four weeks later, and just when I'd given up expecting any reply from his lordship, he rings me out of the blue like, and apologises; telling me his wife is just about to have their third baby and could I give him a ring in five or six weeks time?

So I says that's fine.

Well, what else could I ruddy well say? Could your wife hold the baby back a few weeks please, whilst I has a few Massage treatments from yer?

And I just resigns meself to the growing tightness in me shoulder and I waits. Them doctors had said there was nothing they could really do about me shoulder, see? As long as I'm lifting our Mickey so much every day.

Well what else am I supposed to do?

Leave the poor fella shitting and pissin' himself on the floor?

And them ruddy social workers weren't that much better, were they? Coming over and showing me how to use a bleeding winch to lift our Mickey - like as if I hadn't been managing fine for the last twenty years - and then they only goes and drops him and breaks his leg, the poor li'l mite.

Can you believe it?

They was only showing me as how I must conform to their Health and Safety regulations.

Health and Safety.

In me own house!

"Well you can sod yer ruddy health and safety," I says to them, "and you can sod yer ruddy winch, too. What about our Mickey's health and safety?"

I'll ruddy well lift him meself, won't I?

Mind you, I can't promise to break his legs like that lot.

Not being a professional, like.

The nosy busy-bodies.

Why can't they get a job annoying somebody else? Why does they always have to keep coming round and picking on us?

I mean, don't they have lives of their own?

It's not like they've done a single friggin' thing to help us with our Mickey in all these twenty years, is it? You wanna know what I thinks?

I thinks them social workers are the saddest bunch of interfering old tossers on the whole planet, I do.

So anyway, where was I?

Oh yeah, his lordship asking me ter wait until they had their third baby - Petey I think they called him - before I gets me appointment...

Well, I waits me six weeks, don't I?

And then I rings him up again and leaves him a message. And then I rings him up again a week later and leaves another message.

And then again a week after that.

Finally, after July has come and almost gone like, he rings back and says he can fit me in at the end of August.

On a Bank Holiday Monday, can you believe?

Well, I says nothing about that 'cos yer know what?

If that's the only day he can do, then I'm gonna be

there, ain't I? He don't half have this posh voice though; feels like I'm talking to the Prime Minister, it does.

All *Lah-dee-dah*, like.

Mind you, it don't seem like his posh voice and education has taught him how to organise himself, does it? Seems to me this here fella couldn't organise a ruddy piss up in a brewery, let alone run an appointment book.

That's what I thinks, anyway.

He can't half massage, though.

I knew he didn't have a clue about that Bank Holiday appointment, so I weren't at all surprised when his lordship rang me up saying as how he were still on holiday in Scotland. He said he was in some strange sounding place called Meaculpa - wherever that is - and can he postpone please, Mavis?

So at last I turns up for me first proper session with him.

In the middle of September.

That's only about six months it's taken to get me appointment. Not bad, eh?

He's not exactly desperate for clients, is he?

Chapter three

So here I am after two hours of driving, standing outside this big posh Victorian house in Halifax in the pouring rain.

Right behind the swimming pool, like.

And I suddenly thinks to meself, what happens now yer daft cow?

'Course I've had plenty of Massages off me mates like, but I ain't never had a proper Massage treatment all to meself, have I?

So I'm right nervous, I am.

I walks up them steps - sandstone steps they are, same as the whole house, like - and I rings the bell. When he opens the big blue door his lordship puts me at ease straight away, doesn't he?

He just looks at me with them blue eyes of his and says - straight out - as how he don't remember me from the course at all.

Ruddy charmin'!

That's a nice technique, I thinks to meself. I should remember that one. How to make yer clients feel at ease, like.

Joking aside though, I'm quite used to it.

Not being noticed, I mean.

I am, honest.

It happens to me all the time, it does. I can chunner on non-stop like this inside me head all day long I can, but I says very little outside.

So most folk don't really notice me at all.

Everyone's so wrapped up in themselves and their own dramas that they're mostly happy not ter have too much competition on the stage floor from yours truly.

So I says very little.

I just lets others do all the talking.

Apart from when I has ter shout at them daft ruddy social workers to protect our Mickey, of course.

Truth is, I feels much better keeping me trap shut.

If yer has ter make a fuss for people to notice you then I thinks, why bother?

I mean like that lady in the lunch queue at Burton Manor after his lordship had given me that first Massage treatment on the course. There she is talking about me and the Massage and I'm only standing right in front of her, aren't I?

The blind old bat.

But I like it that way, I do.

Keeping to meself I mean.

Anyway,

What I do remember from that first session with his lordship in Halifax - apart from him telling me he don't remember me - is him spending *ages* asking me all sorts of questions in this big room downstairs what's full of floral sofas and large cushions. And him writing all me answers down on a fancy laptop.

I remembers him sitting there in his black vest and black flared trousers - all knees and feet - in one of them squashy sofas hunched up over his tiny little laptop.

All I can really see is his great big feet.

One in a blue sock and one in a black sock.

Bless

Then there's his lower legs and I can see these great big knobbly knees through them trousers. Then his laptop and above that his handsome baby-face. And finally, right on the top like, he's got this shock of black hair sticking up at the front, you know, like what *Tin-Tin* had.

But black instead of blond.

Obviously.

Anyway, he's asking for me age and I'm thinking, mind yer own business, mate!

But I tells him don't I?

And then he asks me what I wants from the Massage; why I've come, like? And I'm tempted to say as how it's been that ruddy long since I started trying ter book a session with him, that I haven't a clue now, have I?

I mean his guess is as good as mine, I reckon.

But he seems such a nice young fella, really.

So instead, I asks for the same feeling as I got that time he gave me a Massage on the course over at Burton Manor. And so he asks me - all posh, like - "What feeling would that be then, Mavis, if you could be a little bit more specific, perhaps?"

And all I wants to say is, well you were there too, mate. Don't yer remember how ruddy *blissed out* I were and how I couldn't even walk in a straight line?

But then he must see so many people like, that he probably don't remember me, does he? So I tells him again, and he seems to remember something 'cos he smiles.

He does have a lovely smile, he does...

Anyway, then he asks me how long that feeling lasted? And when I tells him I felt all loose for about six weeks, he sucks in this breath and looks a bit shocked.

So, I'm wondering if there's summat wrong with me, like?

Then he takes me upstairs and he's saying to get on the Massage table and not to worry about him walking in while I'm undressing and all that, 'cos he'll knock first...

I mean, like I'm bothered.

At my age

Chapter four

It's a lovely little room, ain't it?

It's got an orange glow all over it from this wooden blind with great big thick slats.

He keeps it real warm, too; so you doesn't want to keep yer clothes on, anyway. It all looks, well, very simple. Just a dark blue carpet and cream walls with all them lovely pictures of whales on them. And he's got this little table for all his oils and nice wooden shelves for his towels. And standing right in the middle is this wooden Massage table all dressed up lovely with towels and pillows, you know? It just feels...

Cosy

So I gets on the Massage table and it's so soft and comfortable I could just lie here and go to sleep for ever, I could.

Honest.

And then he knocks on the door all polite like, and asks if I'm on the table and I wants ter say, no, I'm levitating in the middle of the room, actually.

But I just says, "Yeah."

And before I knows it, he's started the Massage and I'm in heaven thinking, who needs valium when you can get this? He's doing me back all deep and flowing like and I'm relaxing real nice after all that talking and then suddenly he says out loud that he remembers me, now.

Out o' the blue, like!

Nice knowing you too, mate!

And then I has a really wicked thought, I does. I thinks as how he probably didn't recognise me with all me clothes on, did he?

So I spends the next five minutes trying me best not to giggle.

Anyways at the end I feels real good and *loose* and he says he wants me to give him a ring in a couple of days; to tell him how I feels, like.

He says something about making sure I don't have any bad reactions to the Massage, like.

So I does.

Ring him, I mean

Chapter five

When I does ring him, I'm tempted to say it's a ruddy miracle!

A ruddy miracle I'm actually speaking to him on the phone, that is.

I mean, I was beginning to think he doesn't actually know how to use his friggin' answerphone. But instead I tells him as how I'm still feeling good and I wants to book another session before the next six months is out, if that's all right with him?

And he laughs, like he's used to a bit of ribbing, so I books another one for a couple of weeks time, don't I?

There is summat real *genuine* about this fella, there really is. Like he's just normal and lives round the corner - for all his lah-dee-dah posh voice!

I have a good feeling about working with him

Chapter six

My first private session with Mavis happened a few weeks after the phone call from Scotland.

It took place in my therapy centre in Halifax; a somewhat shabby building I share with my psychotherapy teacher, Richard. It has a training room, a couple of group therapy rooms and a small but cosy Massage room at the top of the stairs.

I love this room; it feels like a cave.

My cave, actually.

It's nothing much, really; just a Massage table and a chair and some shelves for my towels and oils and my CD-player. The thick wooden blinds give the room an earthy feel, they do.

But it's my cave, it is. Just for me and my clients. No one else uses it.

No *contamination*, see?

Sometimes when I walk into this room I think I can still smell all the good work and feel the good energy from everything that has happened in here. Maybe some rooms do that; accumulate and store echoes of what has gone on before...

I think my clients feel it too, because sometimes they get on the table and they have already started their work of releasing tension before I even walk in. It's as if the room has built up an energy all of its own - an atmosphere. It's a bit like when you walk from a bustling city centre street into the still peace of a cathedral.

Makes me stop and breathe, it does.

But first I take a case history from my new clients in the training room downstairs. I like this space for talking; it's nice and light and airy. When I first opened the door to let Mavis in, it was pouring with rain and I still only had the vaguest recollection of her from the course in Burton Manor. In truth, she has a rather plain appearance and is not someone who

15

stands out. She's wearing a see-through Mac and I can see she is dressed in beige trousers with a fisherman's pale blue smock on top.

And sandals. In the pouring rain.

Sandals.

During the case history I learn that after training to be a school teacher, Mavis has pretty much spent her whole life being a devoted wife and mother. She has two very talented daughters who are now grown up. Then there is Mickey, her adopted son:

"Our Mickey has cerebral palsy", she explains to me, smiling, "and this means he only really has the physical and mental functions of a six month old baby, see?"

"Right. Ah... Good. Yes... I think I do see."

I pause, trying to get my head around this information.

Did she say adopted?

"Actually, I haven't the faintest clue!" I confess, smiling at her. "So tell me if you would be so kind, how this affects your ah, day-to-day life then?"

I hate it, really.

All this *peeping Tom* stuff.

But I really do need to have a picture or two of her life before I actually start to massage her. It helps me to feel connected. The trouble is; I am also a passionate believer in *privacy*.

Dear old Mavis does her best to hide any discomfort at my *prying* and says,

"Well, he's almost thirty, see."

Her voice softens as she talks about 'our Mickey'.

"Let's think. How can I explain it to yer?"

She looks around the room at all the large pastel cushions scattered around on the thick green carpet. The staple diet of any therapy centre these large coloured cushions but I do wonder what she makes of them? Should I explain that the other half of my week is spent as a psychotherapist?

"Well," she starts, "first he needs his nappy changing, and then I has to wash and dress and feed him, obviously, but really he needs lots of cuddles and playing with just like a big baby, yer know? And then of course there's all the lifting..."

"So how much lifting would that be exactly, Mavis?" I interrupt. "That you have to do with 'our Mickey' each day, I mean?"

I am already getting the distinct impression that this Mavis wouldn't complain even if she had to rebuild her own house every day, brick by brick. Like dear old Sysiphus, pushing the stone up the mountain-side just for it to roll all the way down again so he has to start over.

Again and again.

But Mavis would do it *cheerfully*, she would.

"Aw loads!" Mavis replies, smiling. "Our Mickey can only drag himself along the floor 'cos his legs don't work at all, see? So I lifts him to wash and dress him and get him in and out of his wheelchair - and all the rest!" She seems *happy* as she says this.

"But I think it's all the lifting that has caused them problems with me shoulder."

"Ah, yes." I say. "Mmm... The *shoulder*. Now, let me see. I believe you mentioned this shoulder in your letter, didn't you?" I pull her letter out of the envelope and scan through it.

"Yes, here it is!" I point triumphantly to the letter where she has written about the shoulder.

"It says here, Mavis - if I may quote you - that you *have been struggling with problems in your shoulder for the last two years*... Super."

Super to actually have the letter with me, is what I mean.

A miracle of efficiency.

For me.

"So tell me," I continue, "what *shoulder* problems would these be then, Mavis?"

She points to her right shoulder and starts rubbing it, saying,

"Well some days, I experiences a real deep ache right here; not sharp, just real deep, you know? On those days, everything I do just *hurts*. I tries and rests, but with our Mickey to sort out all the time, it ain't easy is it?" She laughs,

"Even pain killers don't make hardly no difference at all,

except ter make me feel groggy and not meself, so I don't bother with them if I can help it."

Not a single hint of complaint.

I am absolutely certain she would never mention any of this if I had not been *prying* into her life. I look at her and smile, saying,

"I see. Sounds like jolly hard work to me!"

She looks at me, smiling patiently.

"Nah, it ain't though. Our Mickey's a treasure, he is. And he makes it all so, well... how can I say it? He makes it all... *real...*"

Her eyes drift out the window,

"...like there ain't no better place to be."

I just look at her silently and breathe out slowly.

Just for a moment I think I glimpse something: a door opening right down the middle of her.

And a light is coming out of Mavis.

A light that could burn us all so clean

"Aw listen to me rabbitin' on about our Mickey!"

The door slams shut and the light is gone.

It's 'business as normal' for Mavis. Shame really. Felt like a good place, it did. And now Mavis is saying, *very cheekily*,

"So when does yer clients actually get a Massage, then? Or does we all have ter wait for another six months?"

Well done Mavis. Like your style, old girl

"Absolutely, but just bear with me one more minute if you would be so kind, Mavis? Is there anything else that you can tell me? To help me get a full picture of your day-to-day life?"

"Apart from me Mickey and me shoulder, you mean?"

"That's right." I nod, smiling.

Mavis looks out the window again. The rain is still splattering against the large bay windows.

"Well, let's think... I does all the books and paperwork for me John's business, you know, letters and invoices and all that stuff. He's an electrician, see? But that don't take any real work at all. I mean it's just sitting at a table doing sums and stuff of an evening, ain't it?"

"Right, yes... of course..." I respond.

Can't think of anything harder to do, actually

But that's it.

The last question.

I'm not going to get any more from Mavis and suddenly I don't want to know any more.

It is time for touch.

"Thank you, Mavis. So then... Just to *recapitulate:* your main reason for coming here is to release your shoulder. Have I got that right?"

She nods her head and says,

"Yeah. It's like I said in me letter; I just wants more of what you gave me that time at Burton Manor. You said I don't relax very well and so I thought I should learn how to do that better - you know, relax like - 'cos I felt so good after that session."

"And another thing..." Mavis says.

The rain is now *pounding* against the windows. I find the noise distracting so I lean forward.

"Yes Mavis? What would that be, then?"

"Your Massage ain't nothing like the Massage I learned last year on me training course."

She shifts in her seat, plants both feet firmly on the ground and looks straight at me. Jaw set.

Challenging me, she is.

I'm not quite sure what to say. Not sure whether this is a statement or a question. Feel embarrassed, actually. There is an awkward pause. I look at my feet...

And notice I am wearing odd socks.

Again.

Damn!

"So tell me, Mavis, what is it exactly that made you decide to learn Massage in the first place?"

Diversionary tactic - you coward, Grant

"Oh?" she looks surprised at the question.

"Well, that's easy I suppose. Our Mickey started going to a day care centre..."

She shifts again in the settee; I really must invest in some decent ones. These cheap floral ones are so flimsy that they collapse at the front. Mavis is trying her best not to slide onto the floor, she is.

"...and then I saw this day-time aromatherapy course at our local college and thought well, why not? Maybe I could help our Mickey by giving him some of those essential oils. So I trained in it all last year. Yer know, just to help our Mickey and fill the gap."

"Gap?" I raise my eyebrows, confused.

Chapter seven

"Well, now me two daughters are both away at University, there's no point just sitting around at home all day missin' them, is there?"

Mavis looks at me from the sofa.
So direct.
So simple.
This is what I envy.
"Right, yes, well of course..."
I'm trying to get my head around her definition of being a *fac totem* to her husband's business and looking after her disabled son, as *"sitting around at home all day".*
Now I'm wondering what else she might do that she hasn't told me.
"I see, yes, of course... So, Mavis do you get to massage er, Mickey much or even have a few clients, perhaps?"
"Oh yeah, he just loves it does our Mickey! I massages him every day 'cos his muscles get so tight and hard. And I gotta couple o' clients too, but that's another thing, ain't it?"
"What's that then, Mavis?"
"Well, me clients ain't gettin' anything like what you gave me on that course." She laughs and says, "So I thought I might as well come along and feel what *real* Massage is supposed to be like!"
She wants to know something.
She's on a quest is our Mavis, no doubt about it.
She has made a round trip of almost a hundred miles for this session along the less-than-friendly M62 from Liverpool. She's felt something and it's asked her some questions, it has.
And she wants to know the answers.
I think she'll find them, too

21

So I get up, saying: "Well, I think that's enough *jaw jaw* for now, don't you? Shall we go on up to the treatment room and begin the Massage?"

Five minutes into the Massage when I come to her arm, I suddenly remember everything from our first session at Burton Manor...

Everything

Chapter eight

I ain't going to this 'ere Massage course at Burton Manor, no ruddy way!

Them social workers have just broken our Mickey's leg, haven't they?

And you can imagine what it's like looking after a grown young man of twenty-seven what can't talk, can't feed himself, is incontinent *and now* - thanks to them ruddy tossers - has his leg stuck in a great big plaster.

I couldn't possibly just leave him with me husband John, neither. He does really well with our Mickey, does John. But well, you know...

He's a fella, ain't he?

No. I ain't going, I says to meself. But our John...

He has other ideas, doesn't he?

He just puts down his newspaper and looks over his glasses at me with that wise old owl look on his face and says as how it will be the last chance for me to have a bit of time just for meself away from our Mickey, you know, because of the broken leg and he reckons that I should go.

"And another thing" John says, smiling at me,

"Our Mickey says he wants you to go to Burton Manor and ter *enjoy the break.*"

He's mad is our John.

He's always saying stuff like as if our Mickey's saying it through him.

Enjoy the break...

Hah-ruddy-hah

I am married to the most wonderful man on the planet, I reckon. He's a really good man and he's wise, is my John.

No really, I mean it.

I mean now I look back, that weekend changed me life it did. So how the ruddy hell could John know that?

But he did, didn't he?

Well, I reads the signs and I knows me John ain't gonna let me stay at home; no matter what I says.

So here I am on Saturday morning driving what I calls me Mickey-mobile, which is this great big van converted to get our Mickey and his wheelchair round the place, and I'm driving to this place called Burton Manor in the Wirral. And I'm thinking to meself, I don't need a ruddy break.

It's our John what needs a ruddy break, is the truth.

Then I has this brain-wave: perhaps I could just take the morning off?

I know.

I'll stay till lunch - they does a good lunch at Burton Manor I'm told - and then I'll come back home in the afternoon and say to our John, "It were all a load of old rubbish". And we'll have a good laugh at all them poncy lah-dee-dah therapists and then we'll take our Mickey out for a nice walk before going to Church for evening Mass.

Yeah.

That's what I'll do.

So when I gets there, this Massage teacher fella is standing at the front of the room and he's wearing these black Chinese-style trousers what only comes halfway down below his knees, and he's got a black vest on his top.

But them trousers!

Well...

They just looks like shrunken pyjamas to me, don't they? And I'm thinking, oh ruddy hell what's he on, then?

The room we're in is beautiful - it's full of wood and bookshelves - and there's a lovely view out of them big bay windows across the fields to the sea. And I can see all the sheep and trees and the sun is shining real bright. And for all his pyjamas, this Massage fella looks, well... a bit *athletic*.

You know?

And I'm thinking as how I hopes we don't have to do any of that yoga stuff, you know, where yer has to stick your legs around your friggin' neck and all that.

But he does move funny, he does.

He sort of *prowls* from side to side as he talks; like a caged tiger. And I don't know if it were a trick of the light or summat, but he seems to be *shimmering*. I know it must sound daft, but that first moment I saw him was mesmerising, is all I can call it.

And another thing.

His legs.

Always bent, they are - even when he just stands still - you know, like he's standing on a trampoline and trying to keep his balance?

And when he opens his gob and talks, it just comes out all creamy and posh, like. And he's obviously nervous but his voice still soothes you.

It kinda just rumbles along gently, like.

And he looks at you with these lovely soft blue eyes...

There's summat about this fella, there is.

Fer all his funny clothes, like.

He's very tanned, he is.

And I were just sitting there wondering to meself where he goes on holiday, like, 'cos I'd just die for a tan like that I would, when I suddenly realises that he's asking if anyone wants to be a client?

And everyone else in the room is obviously too scared of him.

Well, I mean...

We don't normally get folk like him around these parts, do we? But I likes him, I does. And then I realises that if I play me cards right I could even get a free Massage from him, have lunch and *then* go home to me John.

He looks like he probably gives a good Massage, you know?

So I does.

Goes and puts up me hand, I mean.

Silly cow that I am

The only trouble were...

That Massage changed me life, didn't it?

It were like being on a train and suddenly the tracks divide up ahead of yer, and all your life you've just been waiting to go on a different track to what you've been going on every day for years and years. Only, you ain't never realised it before...

And then yer does.

Go the other way, I mean

Chapter nine

The Massage were ruddy great, see? I loved every friggin' second of it, I did.

It were like I could feel summat in me body going, "Hello then, what took you so long to arrive, like?"

It were like summat deep in me bones just woke up for the first time in me life. Don't get me wrong, though, 'cos I have a great life, I does. I loves every bit of it, even fighting with them ruddy tossers from social services!

But it were like I'd never had a Massage before... never been touched before.

I thought I'd ruddy died and gone to heaven, I did.

And I felt wondrous soft and loose at the end. Anyway, I dunno whose body he had given me at the end.

But it weren't mine, I can tell you that.

Mind you, I were a bit put out later on when one of them snooty therapy-ladies said to him that I was obviously a Massage therapist and so was all relaxed anyway like, but how well would it work on *real* clients?

Real clients!

Well thank you very much... what the ruddy hell does she think I am, the friggin' woman from Mars, then?

And you know what?

I has to laugh, 'cos this polite young Massage fella almost chokes himself with his cuppa tea when she seys that and his baby-face goes all red like he's having a ruddy fit an' all!

I remember, 'cos the whole coffee room went quiet and looked at him, didn't it? There were loads of people there in the break 'cos there was another course going on in the Manor with that funny little fat fella from the TV, you know? Him what comes on late at night and talks about all the stars and astronomy stuff... oh, wot's his name?

Patrick Moore!

That's right, Patrick Moore.

Anyway, this little fat TV fella's all dressed up in a blue floral shirt like he was on holiday in the ruddy Bahamas or summat, and he's standing right there just a few feet away from us looking all perplexed at this Massage fella wearing pyjamas wot's gotta face that's ready to go super-nova, ain't it?

I thought his lordship were gonna kill the snooty-nose old bat what asked him as how it would work on *real clients.*

I did, 'onest.

But then I were right put out 'cos instead of killing her, like, he went and told her I weren't at all relaxed and that me arm defied Sir Isaac Newton himself.

The cheeky begger!

I don't know what the ruddy hell he meant 'cos I felt so good and relaxed.

You know?

Later on, when I asks me mate Kathy what he meant by that, she says that this here teacher fella pulled some real funny faces when he was working on me arms during the Massage treatment.

"What sort of funny faces?" I asked

"Well, you know..." Kathy said, "Like as if he had eaten something nasty."

That's nice.

So then I'm standing in the queue for lunch and I overhears this woman behind me saying,

"Well! I almost died when he climbed up onto the table to massage her back!"

I turns to her and says, "he did *what?"*

And she tells me as how he climbed up onto the table so his knees were each side of me head and then he goes and does me back *from above!*

Now, I had no idea he'd done nothing like that, did I? And I'm thinking what else did he do that I should know about? So I decides to stay for the afternoon; just to find

28

out, like.

Climbing over me ruddy head indeed!

During the afternoon session I keeps thinking about how good I felt after his treatment. It's like I've got oil in all me joints and all me movements feel smooth.

I wish I could make me own clients feel like this.

And on Sunday I comes back again, don't I?

You know, to make sure I learns how to do that kneeling thing right up on the table, like. And after that weekend I starts doing it on all me clients; 'cos I'm too thick to remember anything else he showed us, aren't I?

And before I ruddy well knows it, people are ringing me up from all around asking if they can come and have one of them deep Massages I give. And then I gets this job at a hospital giving all the staff a Massage and soon I'm booked up for three months.

Three months... Me, Mavis Brown!

Chapter ten

After that I keeps thinking to meself how good me shoulder feels and how little pain I'm feeling there. Not only that; I feels good all over since that Massage.

And I starts to get this idea wot won't go away, will it?

I starts thinking as how I ain't never booked in a Massage just for meself, I ain't.

The only Massage I ever got was when I was on me Aromatherapy course, and some of them girls were worse than me - and that's really saying something!

And so I keeps thinking what would it be like to book a session you know, just for meself like?

A proper session with his lordship.

And I thinks as how I could probably do with some more of that, especially before me shoulder starts to tighten up and hurt again.

So I talks to me John about it and he says I should definitely go for another session if it helps me that much and as how it might help our Mickey too, if I don't get meself injured.

We both dreads havin' to call in them daft bats from social services to help us out. God help our poor Mickey if they ever gets their stupid ruddy hands on him, is all I can say.

So I does, doesn't I? I rings this Massage fella up

Chapter eleven

Mavis' first treatment was my very first public Massage treatment, actually.

It was in Will Gladstone's old hunting lodge, set deep in the Wirral peninsular.

Now don't get me wrong; I don't normally give Massage treatments in baronial settings, but it is an educational establishment and they had asked me to teach my approach. So that's why I am here in dear old Will's hunting lodge standing in front of twelve complete strangers.

How on Earth did you end up agreeing to this, old boy?

We're in a first floor room looking out over the beautiful gardens.

We get a wonderful view.

The dedication that these gardeners must have put into this place over the years... The lawn is divided up into four beautiful sections with a thin rectangular pond in the centre. Each section of the lawn is surrounded by chest-high hedges, like a sort of square maze. And inside each of these four gardens there are stunning flower displays.

Here in the room we are spoilt, too.

It's got a lovely polished wooden floor and the walls are covered in bookshelves.

Gladstone probably read these books

I take a nice deep breath.

The name of the room is fittingly, *the Mersey*. In the distance I can actually see the sea. I rub my hands together and say:

"Hello there. Um, well... my name's Grant and it really is jolly nice to meet you all. Look forward to hearing all about your work and what you get up to, actually."

I look up, smiling hopefully.

Blank faces. Not even a smile for this old boy.

"Don't get allowed out much, see?" I smile again. Not a flicker of response at my joke.

"Well, what I mean by that is, what with clients and family, I don't get the chance to meet other therapists that much." I smile at them.

You know what, Grant? It's just possible you are in the wrong room and this is the flower painting group

I breathe again.

"So, welcome to my very first course about all this stuff. Don't suppose you've got much of a clue what 'this stuff' is about though, have you? Not sure I have either, to tell you the truth."

I chuckle and look at the floor.

When I look up...

More stone faces.

Actually, come to think of it a stone wall would have *a lot* more expression. They look like refugees who ended up in the wrong country.

Can't speak the lingo, by the look of things.

Focus, Grant
Breathe
Connect with your belly...

"So," I continue, "what do you say to me giving an actual Massage treatment, right here, right now in front of you? So you can see what it is I do, actually? Anyone like that idea, before we have coffee, perhaps?"

A definite response here.

Almost everyone is nodding their head now.

Well done, old boy, seems like you might have found the right room after all

"Oh good show! So what I need is a *client*, then. Not a 'model', mind."

I trace the apostrophes in the air with my fingers,

"Must confess, I don't know how to massage a 'model', see? Everything I do has come through doing *actual* treatments on *real* clients over the last ten years, so it

32

must be someone who actually wants a treatment... anyone game, perhaps?"

Blank faces.

No volunteers.

They are a nervous bunch, this lot.

Give them time...

I can hear the gardeners whistling and talking to each other outside the windows, planting yet another set of their amazing flower displays.

What a setting for my first course, eh?

I glance out of the window and can see the sun shining out from behind the clouds onto the blossom of the oak trees that surround this idyllic manor.

And in the distance, the sea.

"So what I mean is this: would anyone actually like to have a Massage, so the others can see what it is I do?"

Maybe I should learn to speak a bit more slowly.

Could be their second language, perhaps?

After a pause that feels like three days, a very solid, middle aged lady smiles at me and says,

"Yeah, go on then, I'll have a Massage."

"Excellent! So what is your name, then? What is it I should call you?"

"Mavis."

Thank you, Mavis
Thank you, Mavis
Thank you, Mavis

Chapter twelve

So I get Mavis onto the table as quickly as I can.

Only once I start does it actually occur to me, that I have never given a live *public* treatment before. They are all crowding close around me, peering over my shoulder, some taking notes. Very aware of them, I am. Not sure what to do, actually.

Beginning to feel a bit invaded.

They are interfering with the Massage

"I say, would you mind awfully taking three steps back, everyone?" I say, "I mean you'll understand why later, but don't just look at my hands. Look at the whole of me, okay? Look at my feet and my legs, perhaps? Might understand more about my approach if you watch them as well, okay?"

They all move back.

"Thanks."

Until now, all my sessions have been done in the privacy of my own treatment room. So I wonder what they must think about my Massage, what it must actually look like?

I begin to feel a bit of a fool, to be honest.

While I am thinking about how *goofy* I must look to the class, the treatment is slipping away from me.

Concentrate on Mavis, Grant
Breathe!

I close my eyes.

Now there is just me and Mavis in the room.

This is what you know about, old boy. Just forget the whole teaching thing, and concentrate on Mavis

Now I am back on *terra firma.*

This I know.

And Mavis is with me, she is. I can hear her breathing

and feel her; muscle and bone. As I move, she moves.

Well done, old girl

Here on the back she gives a little and moves with me. This is a strong back.

She may be small but this back feels very compact. Brimming with strength, it is. Here in the hips there is quite a lot of movement, too. When I apply pressure the hips *give*.

Roll, they do.

But up here by the neck and the shoulder we have a different feel. This feels very solid, *rock solid,* not to put too fine a point on it. Our Mavis feels *held,* as in 'held tight'. And when I try and move her arms, they only move under great pressure.

Slowly.

The primary image I get is that I am pushing against gates that are *rusted.*

The thing I remember most from this first session with Mavis is lifting her elbow off the pillow to work on her arm (she is lying face down with her arms hanging off the table) and then releasing it gently so that it can fall back down again.

But with Mavis, instead of her arm gently lowering onto the table as I slip my hand away, her arm just stays there suspended in mid air.

It seems to grin at me and say,

"So you thought you actually knew something about Massage, did you?"

I have massaged some pretty tense people in my career so far, but I have *never* seen anyone leave their arm hanging suspended like this.

My first public treatment, and I have to get a client whose body actually defies the laws of gravity

I slowly push her arm back down to the table, thinking that here is something probably worth exploring.

Very much so.

Quite remarkable it is, this arm. Despite my frustration I am intrigued at what would make her do this with her arm.

35

Nevertheless, I have an *instinct* to politely pass on by.

To continue on with the Massage as if nothing has happened. After all, I have no agreement to give Mavis anything more than a simple Massage, do I?

No *explicit contract* to go exploring anything deep or personal at all, eh?

No prying, see?

Chapter thirteen

They speak a strong language, here in this land

So I continue on with the treatment, learning more about the contours of Mavis' body and doing my best to learn the language it speaks. It is a *responsive* language; one eager to learn new words and absorb new ideas.

The people that live in this land - the land of Mavis' body - are *open*, they are.

Yet I am troubled.

It feels like here is a language without any words of *doubt*. I do love this strong accent and rich words, don't get me wrong. There is a security in this certainty that I personally crave.

But I am missing something, I am.

Right here in the *feel* of Mavis, I am missing some of the depth and sensitivity that comes hand in hand with doubt.

An acceptance of our inherent *frailty* is what I'm missing. I think fragility and doubt are our birthright actually; just as much as strength and certainty.

We need our poor Hamlet just as much as we need our dear old King Harry the fifth. I'm rather a fan of the tortured musings of our young Hamlet, truth be told. In the spaces that such doubt creates, I find new and deeper insights emerge for me...

So I continue on with the treatment, the *intrigue* of her floating arm notwithstanding. Mavis is an excellent client. She does everything in her power to let in the touch.

She is a good sport, is our Mavis

After the session, she walks around the table; actually she *glides* around the table. She seems deeply affected by the treatment and reports feeling very "loose". What I notice is that she is smiling more and her eyes have a real sparkle about them.

The group sees that there is quite a change, too.

During the coffee break in this plush lounge downstairs, the therapists all gather round me; it is crowded with another course. They start to ask me questions.

Excited, they are.

One of them, a tall lady with tight hair and glasses, looks down at me and says rather *expertly*,

"Obviously it looked okay on her, but then she was very relaxed wasn't she? Would it work with a *real* client?"

Not sure I heard her right.

Relaxed, she said

"Relaxed!" I splutter into my teacup, "I say old thing, didn't you see her arm suspended in mid air - like it was defying Sir Isaac Newton himself?"

The group laughs, but I notice Mavis' face drop.

Damn! You were so busy pressing home your righteousness, Grant, that you just forgot the feelings of the most important person in the room - Mavis

I turn to her and squeeze her arm, saying,

"Listen, Mavis, don't take any notice of what this old boy says. Truth is this: I think you did a *heroic* job on that table, back there. Never easy when being watched by strangers! You were a super-hero to me actually, Mavis. Work with you again any day, I would. Fantastic breathing. Did everything perfectly. Tension like that can happen any time. Main thing is this; you let it go. Still feeling loose, are we, Mavis?"

Mavis smiles, nodding, looking relieved.

Remember her first session?

I should think so

Chapter fourteen

I'm getting the hang of all this 'ere Massage stuff, I am.

I'm all cosy lying on this Massage table wrapped up in towels, aren't I? I'm lying face down with me head turned to the side so's I can see this beautiful picture of a whale leaping outta the water. And here I am thinking like I knows what's coming, don't I?

It's me third session so I'm an expert now, ain't I?

Only his lordship goes and does something totally different, don't he?

Instead of starting off like the last two times, he just puts his hand on me lower back without so much as a "how d'yer do?" and suddenly I'm just melting, I am...

It's uncanny.

He keeps doing this for ruddy ages, you know, saying nothing! And the warmth in his hands just goes right through me whole body.

I'm away with the fairies, me

Then, out of the blue he says that he's sure I didn't come here just to lie like this... and I'm thinking, this is ruddy marvellous, mate! You can keep doing this all friggin' day if yer wants...

But that probably isn't the right answer, is it?

So I just mumbles something about as how me head feels twenty-one but me body still thinks I'm fifty-three, so could he please get me body to feel twenty-one as well, like?

Now I'm only joking, ain't I?

But his lordship thinks I'm being serious and he says, all pompous like, that he "Can't agree to a *contract* like that, because you can never fool the body, Mavis." And I thinks, oh ruddy hell, so now we're doing contracts are we, your royal lah-dee-dah-ness?

I don't remember buying no house nor signing no contracts, neither...

Anyroads, I don't care 'cos I'm just drifting off with the fairies, me. And I wanna ask him where it says in the small print that I would end up feeling like ruddy melted cheese on toast, then?
But instead I says nowt and just floats away...

I think he finally gets it, you know, that I'm dead and pissed all at the same time.
'Cos he mutters summat about "just seeing what emerges." Well I'll tell you what emerges: what emerges is me flying away like a ruddy butterfly, mate.
I don't remember what I said at the end of the Massage but I never knew it were possible to feel so loose all over me body. Me legs were like ruddy jelly and I'm just sliding along the pavement as I walks to me van, ain't I?
And in me head I'm feeling, well, "chilled" as me daughters would say but more'n that really. It's like whatever happens, everything is gonna be all right.
Yeah, that's right.
Everything's *cooooool*, man.
So he asks me to give him a ring after a couple of days again, which I do and I tells him I still feels great but could I have another session before the next millennium is out, please?
He laughs again, you know, like he knows I ain't never gonna let him forget how hard he made it for me to have that first session.

So I books another one, don't I?

Chapter fifteen

We're having a bad day aren't we, old sport?

It happens.

The demons come to visit and they go round smashing up the furniture in my head, so to speak.

Mavis is on the table and I'm just standing there with my hand on her lower back, hoping she won't hear all the commotion going on in my head.

Once again I wonder what it is I'm actually doing here.

Could somebody tell me, please?

It feels strange finding myself here, right here actually. I mean living the part of a therapist, when all I really feel is that I should be locked up in dear old Salem House for screaming lunatics.

But I'm not, am I?

By the grace of God I am here in my cave in Halifax.

I have food in my belly and a roof over my head and no one is pointing a gun at me, are they? I mean, what have I possibly got to complain about?

But these demons just won't go away, will they?

So here I am and it's the first Massage of the day and this is Mavis.

And she is a good one, this Mavis.

A real nugget

When the demons come to visit like this I just don't feel in any way *worthy* of the good people like Mavis who come to see me and place their trust in my touch. I know I should get into the flow of the thing, but I feel so damned useless, I simply can't move.

Voices, see?

Voices screaming at me actually

Telling me what a fool I am and how no one will ever

take me seriously - what an utter idiot I am.

Absolutely true, see?

As a distraction from these voices, I ask Mavis what she wants from the treatment. But she makes no reply whatsoever.

So I just wait. And wait.

And wait.

Mavis says *absolutely nothing.*

It's a dull day outside and the wooden blinds give the room a very dark feel, today. The fan heater whirrs noisily.

I feel irritable.

Well I'm trying to block out the screaming demons in my head, okay?

"Now Mavis, I'm sure you didn't come here just to lie like this on the table, did you? So tell me, if you would be so kind, what it is you want from the session today?"

She mumbles something ridiculous about wanting her body to feel twenty-one.

Don't you understand that the demons are ripping down the curtains, smashing down the walls and screaming at me, Mavis?

So I reply: "Well, the thing is, Mavis..."

The demons cackle away, gesturing obscenities at me

"...Can't fool the body like that, I'm afraid. I wonder... anything a bit more down to Earth that you want from this treatment? Anything I could actually deliver, perhaps?"

I'm holding up the walls here, Mavis

Can you help me out just a little?

Not a good day to be playing games, I'm afraid

I need something solid to get us going, old girl

She says nothing.

Anything solid for me at all, Mavis? Because I could really use some help here, not to put too fine a point on it

She turns her head, sighs and well...

Says nothing.

Really need to get moving, we do, Mavis, before these demons take up permanent residence

And then I suddenly get it!

She's halfway into the treatment already and like a damned fool I haven't realised it.

The old girl's jumped ship without even telling me, or rather, I've been so busy thinking about these stupid demons in my head I didn't notice her going over the side, did I?

"Okay Mavis," I say, "we will just have to see what happens... That okay with you?" She nods her head.

Contract achieved
Go! Move!
Don't lose her!
But she's already gone deep, has our Mavis.
I'll have to move quickly to catch her...

I'm throwing myself off the side of a boat in slow motion. I feel myself flying through the air, and then I am cutting into the water like a sword and reaching down, swimming through the water so fast and reaching out with my hand, straining as hard as I can... I have to find her!

On the surface, back at the Massage table, I sink deeper and deeper into my breath and do my best to feel my belly and my whole body... I press my weight into my feet.

I can see her!
A distant small brown shape hurtling down into the dark waters below me. I speed up. Swim faster, dammit! I must reach her. My arm is stretching out, reaching, reaching... and...
Contact!
I grab Mavis' foot
There!
I am with you. We do this together, okay Mavis?
No solo dives... not quite yet old girl

Back at the Massage table I suddenly feel a connection between my movements and Mavis' body. I feel that her breath is all around me.

Like a blind dancer, I can feel her every movement through my whole being...

Deep down in the dark, with the water rushing past us, she smiles up at me and dives deeper - I stay close. We are going down... While the demons are screaming through my head up on the surface like a distant storm, Mavis and I swim deeper and deeper into the dark ocean
Together
I am happy now...

Back on the surface, something feels different, now that I am actually connecting with Mavis. Something is *loosening*. Her body seems to be responding to the touch and she is beginning to really move.

She is becoming fluid is our Mavis. The rocks are turning into jelly...

Finally we reach it
This place I know so well: the place of swirling currents
Suddenly, down here deep in the ocean, we are dragged sideways and then sucked backwards, tossed over and over, tumbling helplessly
We are like holy St. Jonah, tossed around in the cavernous belly of the whale
There is a moment of panic in Mavis and I just reach out and grab her hand to say that it's okay
Strange, but okay
Been here many times before old girl, so don't worry.
Thing is not to fight it - give yourself over to it
And she does, bless her
She just lets go and so we tumble endlessly in the maelstrom, looking like two tiny specks of dust in the vast swirling ocean currents, Mavis and I...

And after what feels like an eternity she turns and faces me and says, "Can we go back home now, please?"
Of course we can
Absolutely, old girl
So I bring her back, oh so gently. I bring her all the way back to the table, I do

At the end of the session here in Halifax, there are no

words; just a deep silence.

A benediction, actually.

The demons have left, thank goodness. The furniture inside my head is a bit of a mess, but I don't mind clearing up because there is such a sense of *relief*.

I could sit in this beautiful silence, forever.

"So what is it you are noticing, then, Mavis?" I ask when she is dressed and walking around the table,

"I mean tell me what you actually feel as you walk right now?"

"I feels like a friggin' piece of jelly!" she laughs, almost keeling over as she walks around the Massage table.

That's exactly what you are, Mavis
A jellyfish
My very own jellyfish - all the way from the Mersey

Chapter sixteen

After walking around like a wobbly old jellyfish, Mavis turns up for her fourth session looking very *loose*.

Softer than I have seen her look at any time before, actually. Which is why I am surprised to find her arm stuck in mid-air again, less than ten minutes into the Massage. This time I can't go politely by, can I? It's beginning to get in the way is this arm.

In fact...

It's beginning to annoy me

Whenever something annoys me like this during a session, I know it can either be the demons in my head or it can be my client's body waving a flag at me saying, "Now! Now is the time."

Knowing the difference though, that's the thing.

Best way to find out is do a reconnaissance fly over.

Come on Biggles, let's go take a peep, eh?

Doing my best to contain my irritation, I say as gently as I can,

"Mavis, could you tell me where you have put our dear old friend Sir Isaac Newton, by any chance? It's just that we seem to have mislaid him again."

Her whole body locks at this transaction.

She stops breathing and opens her eyes to look at me, confused. The whirr of the fan heater seems very loud suddenly. Her eyes look out at me from the side of the Massage table.

Well that worked well didn't it Biggles old boy? So much for taking a quiet peep, eh?

Better push on - now that I've been spotted, so to speak,

"I mean we seem to be defying the laws of gravity, Mavis, right here with this arm."

46

I decide to play the clown and start lifting the towel by her feet as if looking for Mr. Newton.

She's still looking at me, confused.

She thinks you've lost the plot, old boy

"Any ideas where you might have put it then, this gravity?" I point to her arm which remains suspended in mid air, even though I have let it go.

She just looks at it, nonplussed.

"Let me help you out, Mavis," I say, holding her arm again, "When I press down like this..." I push gently but definitely on her arm, "Can you *feel* how you are holding it up here, perhaps? Yes?"

As I press down, the arm begins to give and slowly lowers; like a hinge that has not been oiled in years. Slowly it touches the table.

When it is fully down I say:

"I think it's probably time to do something rather different, Mavis. Time to take some *direct action* with this arm of yours. What I suggest for today's session is working on your whole body through this arm. Like me to say a little bit more about this?"

"Go on, then" she replies.

"Well, it's like this..." I look up, startled.

The room has suddenly gone dark. The sun must have just gone in because the blinds can do that, they can. Mavis' face has gone into shadow.

A bit spooky, actually.

"This is what we call a *holding pattern*, it is." I continue. "And it's not really your arm at all - nothing wrong with the muscles - nice and soft, see?"

I squeeze her upper arm.

"It's the way your brain has learned to hold your arm. Bit of a *habit* is what we've got here, Mavis. So by focusing on this holding pattern we can help your brain to take it easy and perhaps soften up a bit; take a bit of a holiday, actually."

She looks puzzled.

"The idea is to retrain your brain to let dear old Sir Isaac do his work again. Let gravity in now and then, so to speak. Thing is, we can't do this *holding pattern* work and massage the whole body at the same time."

"So you means I won't be getting no Massage at all, then?" Mavis asks, looking confused.

"Not in the strictest sense of the word, no. But we still use the touch to see if you can let go a little, here in the arm. As you let go in your arm, you let go all over. It's really the brain that is loosening, you see."

"You mean... like it's a *brain Massage?*"

"Well yes, I suppose you could say that, couldn't you? Jolly good description, actually. Brain Massage. Mmm... might use that description myself."

"Be my guest." she replies quietly.

Very *dry* our Mavis can be, when she wants to.

"So I won't be working all over your body with the oils like before, Mavis, but you should feel the effects of this in your whole body. Bit different from all our other work - fancy a go?"

"Yeah, all right, let's go for it." She says, "What d'ya want me to do?"

Contract acquired, old boy

I grab my wooden stool like an eager little boy running up to the ice cream van and sit down close to her head at the side of the table.

Here we go, then...

Take your time, Grant old boy

Go slow

"Okay, Mavis, so just close your eyes and feel me lifting your arm just a couple of inches off the table."

I lift her arm slowly.

"There, feel that?" She nods.

"Now when I let go just let the weight of the arm itself take it back down to the table. My hands will be ready to catch it, so don't worry about that."

I wait a while and then...

I move my hands away so her arm can fall down towards the table again.

But her arm just stays there, suspended in mid-air.

Held up by string, it seems...

"So let me help you out here, Mavis. Open your eyes if

you would?" She looks at her arm.

Unblinking and uncomprehending.

"See the gap here, Mavis, between your arm and the table?" I twiddle my finger up and down in the space between her arm and the table, "Shouldn't really be here, this gap, see? Could you just let the arm drop down, perhaps?" She pushes her arm down onto the table with a thud.

As if pushing down a plunger.

I close my eyes and take a deep breath.

This is not going to be easy. Not easy at all

I ask Mavis to turn over so she is lying on her back.

"Okay, Mavis, what I'm going to do now is take over your arm. I want you to give it to dear old Uncle Grant, if you don't mind. Play *possum* for a bit, would you, Mavis? I will tell you when you are holding and when you let go."

I look around the room and my eye falls on my picture of the leaping Orca whale, half out of the water; the light catching his body as he begins to fall back into the water.

"Thing is, I don't want you to help me at all. Don't want you to do anything at all, see? Want you to let your arm fall down back into the water like that great heavy whale, see? I want gravity to take your arm down, all free of charge."

I smile and add, "Special offer on Wednesdays, see?" I smile, pleased at my little joke.

She opens one eye and says, dry as a desert,

"It's Thursday."

Good show, Mavis

We both laugh at this and...

Hey presto, the arm flies even higher, doesn't it? Her arm is now floating out to the side of the table like lady Godiva proffering her hand for me to kiss.

So much for laughter therapy helping her to release...

She sees this floating arm of hers and points to it with her other arm and starts laughing even more. Before we know it we are both crying with laughter.

Getting hysterical we are, actually.

Laughing helplessly at this absurd *anti-gravity* arm of hers.

After we have both calmed down we start again.

I lift her arm and then I let it go.

Again and again.

My irritation has left me completely now we are *on task*. I move her arm and whenever she gives me her weight I tell her and whenever she takes it back, I tell her.

It is slow hard work, particularly for Mavis.

After a while I don't have to verbalise it so much as she begins to feel herself taking control and then letting go. A silence descends; full of concentration.

Now we are silent dancers, Mavis and I...

There's nothing particularly strange about Mavis' holding.

We all do it.

It's just that with Mavis it is... well, a bit *extreme*. These holding patterns are almost invisible during normal life, but once we are lying on a Massage table they are very hard to hide.

With Mavis lying on her back I am able to try out a whole range of different arm positions and movements. I have to close my eyes to feel the difference between when she is loose and when she takes back control.

Every time I feel her start to anticipate my movements I go in a different direction.

Like cat and mouse, we are.

I mean it's completely safe for her to give me her arm, isn't it?

Totally safe.

Yet she cannot do it - not completely, anyway. But you know what?

Towards the end of the session, I feel Mavis making real progress, really letting go, and I am able to make both small and large movements of her arm without any resistance at all. When I am doing this the rest of her body and even her head seem to sink deeper into the table.

The atmosphere in the room changes from furrowed brow and intense concentration to heaviness; as if she has gone unconscious.

Wherever Mavis needed to go today, she is there.

I feel lighter and breathe a nice deep, easy breath. I look around the room and realise the sun must have come out sometime in the last thirty minutes because the whole room is now glowing a deep *orange*.

And Mavis?

Well, Mavis' face is looking golden, actually.

Afterwards, once she is dressed, she looks bewildered and astonished.

It really does look like she doesn't know how to walk.

For a long time she just stands there, as if she is not quite sure which foot to step forward with. Slowly, she starts to move and there is a sense of her feet floating off the floor every time she lifts them.

She looks like she's in space does our Mavis. Not in space, I realise.

Exploring gravity.

Mavis is exploring gravity, she is

She does this moonwalk for quite a while.

Once she starts moving more easily, albeit totally differently, I ask her about the *feel* of this walk and she starts to fill up with tears, does our Mavis.

There is a dam inside, and it looks like breaking at any moment

But Mavis just shakes her head and busies herself packing up her things and leaves. I remember asking her if she was okay to drive all the way back to Liverpool as she walked past me, but she was in too much of a hurry to answer.

I wonder what she was about to say?

Still, mustn't push things...

Not today

Chapter seventeen

At me next Massage - me fourth I'm on now - right in the middle, you know, just when I'm feeling all melted again, he suddenly stops and asks me what have I done with gravity, like?

So I opens me eyes and there's me arm not resting on the table at all but just floating there. He's not even touching it, see, and he's telling me to just let go but it doesn't wanna move.

I'm looking at it in confusion, I am, and he must have seen that 'cos he asks me, all posh like, "if we can focus on this today, perhaps, Mavis?"

He says it's something called me holding patterns and that instead of Massaging all over me body, he wants to work on me whole body just through me arm, like.

Well, I ain't got a friggin' clue what he's going on about, have I?

Holding patterns, indeed.

And then he starts talking about doing a ruddy brain Massage as well!

I do wonder if he's on something, I really do.

But of course I agrees to whatever he says - I mean he's the boss, ain't he?

So he just holds me arm and keeps asking me if I'm holding it up or if it's him what's holding it up. I mean, you think he'd know without me having ter tell him, wouldn't yer?

Him being a Bodyworker an' all.

And anyway, sometimes it's him and sometimes it's me what's holding it up - apparently - and you know what? Most of the time I can't even tell the difference, can I?

And there was me thinking I was normal, like.

So now it's worse, ain't it? I'm tensing up throughout me whole body trying not to ruddy help him and to "let go" of me arm, you know? And he's beginning to look like he might start blowing steam outta his ears 'cos I can't do it, like.

So after I turns over, he says to "Just let it drop, Mavis" and then just as I'm thinking I was all nice and relaxed I opens me eyes and there's me arm floatin' above me friggin' head by the ceiling like a barrage balloon in the ruddy blitz!

And him not even touching it, neither.

Well that just sets us both off laughing, don't it?

And that seems to relax him a little; well, I tries me best to help the poor fella, don't I? I mean he looks like he works far too hard, what with his nice young family an' all. Anyway, he's ever so nice and he says "not to worry", when I says how hard it is to let go and he says that it's just them holding patterns.

So that's all right then, isn't it?

I suppose.

And he keeps telling me over and over to just "breathe and feel" which I reckon is what all these therapist fellas say when what they really wants is for you to shut your ruddy trap so they can get on with the job!

So I does.

Shuts me trap, I mean.

And anyways, I'm lying here all confused and thinking to meself, what the ruddy hell is he on about "holding patterns"; I mean, what's an holding pattern when it's at home, like?

And then I'm wondering, maybe it's the same as me knitting patterns? And then when I thinks about it, I reckon I probably have dropped a stitch or two in me time, haven't I?

So it's probably the same with me brain, ain't it? And now I'm giggling to meself 'cos I'm thinking, Mavis Brown, you're definitely a few stitches short of a pattern, you!

Then his lordship says to "Breathe" all serious, like, so I just translates that into "Shut your ruddy gob, Mavis" but what with me stitches being dropped and him being so posh and polite like, I can't hardly stop myself from giggling now, can I?

And then he must think I'm crying or summat 'cos me whole body must be shaking as I'm giggling, like, and he says all sympathetic and gentle, like, for me to just "let it all out, Mavis" and as how it's good ter "let go" and now I'm in agony 'cos I'm ruddy 'owling inside.

He's being so ruddy serious and the more serious he is the funnier it gets, you know? Like when you're in church and you gets the giggles.

And he ain't gotta friggin' clue, has he?

Well, he does take himself a bit too serious, like, doesn't he?

Bless him.

He probably had a bad night with that new baby of his.

So I calms down and starts to breeeeeathe, you know? Just like what I'm supposed to do and for all me giggling, I realises I'm tensed up all over and I'm only holding me arm up in the air again, aren't I?

And he just keeps talking to me, doing this same thing over and over, telling me when I'm holding me arm up all by meself and when I lets it go...

He's ever so patient

His voice is real soft and encouraging; like he could do this all day long. Well he probably does, doesn't he, yer daft cow? 'Cos this is his ruddy job, ain't it?

How thick can you get?

Anyway the feel of his touch is so, well...

Encouragin'

And I keeps peeping me eyes open, ter see if it's him or me what's holding up me arm - 'cos I know he don't like it when I has me eyes open, like - and there he is, sitting on that little stool of his with his eyes all closed and his baby-face all serious and scrunched up like.

He's wearing this black vest and these big baggy balloon trousers what is all black and he's breathing out real loud, like he's doing an imitation of a steam train.

So here I am just lying on me back looking at the peeling and cracked ceiling above me head, doing me best to "let go" but what I'm really thinking is "he definitely needs a decorator in here, he does..."

Now I'm not quite sure what he did, but I just remembers how one minute I'm lying there thinking about all this holding pattern stuff and me knitting needles, you know?

And I'm looking at his cracked ceiling and thinking as how, what with the way he's breathing out all loud and funny like, if I'm one stitch short of a pattern, then he's definitely got more cracks up top than is good for him, hasn't he? So I'm just lying here thinking all that stuff and then the next minute, well, everything goes very strange, it does...

I mean, one minute he's moving me friggin' arm and then the next moment I ain't looking at the ceiling anymore, am I?

Everything's a blur

And I'm ruddy well going through it, I am; the ceiling, that is. And I keeps going up through the roof and up above this posh Victorian house, like...

And I'm spinning and tumbling all over the friggin' place, I am

I ain't on a massage table at all, I ain't

'Cos that's far below me, now

And I'm flying through the sky above Halifax and he's just throwing me around all over the ruddy place and spinning me upside down like I'm a tiny insect in these giant ruddy hands of his and while I'm spinning all I can hear is his voice saying:

"That's it, Mavis. Now you're letting go, well done, old girl!"

And I thinks, hey, less of the 'old' if you don't mind, but I can't say 'owt, can I? 'Cos me mouth's still on the table down there and I'm ruddy miles above Halifax up here in the sky

And these big hands of his are just tossing me about the place and each time he throws me up it's like I'm gonna fall to me death it is, and I'm thinking,

I'm gonna die here, I am

But then I hears his voice calmly telling me to keep breathing and just to trust him and he keeps catching me and then tossing me up in the air again and again, doesn't he?

And I know it sounds ruddy daft but that's what's happening, 'cos, like... well I know he's only moving me arm but it's me whole body what's being thrown around all over the place

Honest

And I'm thinking,

"Maybe this is what it feels like when yer takes them hallucinogenic drugs, like?

And before I know it he's saying,

"Okay Mavis, get dressed when you're ready, okay?"

Ready? Me?

You gotta be joking!

'Cos I just feels like a bag o' bones on the table and, well, like I ain't got no ruddy muscles at all, neither.

So I'm lying here thinking as how this is what it must be like to be paralysed from the neck down; me whole body feels so heavy, like I'm made of lead...

Maybe he broke me neck when I wasn't looking?

So I turns me head from one side to the other and it seems to work okay.

And then I moves me fingers and toes 'cos I remembers that's what doctors tell folk to do in them films when someone has broken their neck, you know?

Anyway, everything works.

So that's good, then, ain't it?

But when I does get dressed and walk around the table, I feels like a ruddy spaceman walking on the moon.

For all me heaviness on the table, me feet feel so *light*, they just wanna float up to the ceiling every step I take and then when he asks me what it's like to walk this way, I suddenly knows I'm just gonna burst into tears.

For no reason that I can understand.

So I just says "fine" and I leaves as quickly as possible

without looking him in the eye.

'Cos I know I'll just start bawling if I looks into those soft blue eyes of his...

Chapter eighteen

So when I rings him a few days later, I tells him as how I've been feeling ruddy awful sometimes, and then ruddy good at other times; and what the hell is that all about, then?

But he doesn't answer, does he?

He just keeps asking me more questions.

So I tells him me shoulder were in real pain for the next day but then, after that, both me shoulders felt really free for the first time in ruddy ages; even better than before. But that's not all, 'cos somehow they feels different, you know?

But it's more than just the shoulders.

It's like a part of me has changed and I feels different. Perhaps not even different; but new. Like something a bit exciting is happening.

Something really good...

I mean, if you'd asked me how I wanted to feel, I would have just said "no pain will do nicely, mate", but this weren't just 'no pain'; it were something else.

It's like me shoulders have a life and a voice all of their own, you know? And I've been ignoring them for years and years... so I asks him if this is normal, and what's going on, like?

And all his lordship says is "not to get stuck in theory, Mavis", but to just tell him what I'm actually experiencing...

So here I am now, me.

Sitting at the bottom of the stairs on a Saturday morning rabbiting on over the phone to his lordship; telling him as how every time I goes out in me Mickey-mobile, I keeps taking the wrong ruddy turning. And me living here, in the same street, doing the same ruddy journey for the last 20 years!

And he just starts laughing and telling me that this is "Absolutely brilliant".

But what's brilliant about that, then?

You know?

And all he's doing is laughing down the other end of the phone and getting all excited and not answering any of me questions.

Well thanks very much, mate.

But he just keeps on laughing, doesn't he?

And it's kind of infectious, his laugh, so I'm laughing too - for no reason that I can understand.

And there he is saying in his posh voice, "Well done" and "Jolly good" and as how this is just me 'holding patterns' starting to release, and as how I'm probably letting go of me scripts and I know I'm laughing, but really I'm just getting more 'n' more confused now, I am.

'Cos I don't know what the friggin' hell he means by scripts, do I?

I mean, I'm still trying to get me head around all these knitting patterns and them mortgage contracts and now he's talking about scripts like I'm auditioning for a friggin' play...

But he does have a lovely laugh, he does

Chapter nineteen

When Mavis turns up for her fifth session she is asking me all sorts of questions, she is.

So I sit down on the Massage table and try to answer them as fully as I can. She's wearing her beige trousers again and a neat brown top with short sleeves. She's sitting in the little wicker chair in the corner of my cave; it's normally only used to throw clothes on before clients dive onto the table.

The trouble is; Mavis is not on the table, is she?

She's asking questions, she is.

The thing about answering Mavis' questions is I need to be very careful not to impose any *interpretation* of mine upon her. If anything, I need to help her to believe in and trust her own experiences more; so she can draw whatever conclusions *she* needs to. After all, it's her session, not mine.

Which is just therapy-speak for me shutting up, really.

But our Mavis is agitated, she is.

So I explain a bit about scripts and how Massage can affect the mind and emotions as well as the body. As I talk she starts to fill up and goes very quiet.

I see she is struggling with me seeing this emotion and suggest we get on with the Massage and she nods her head in relief.

The Massage starts very normally; just a regular old Massage.

When she turns onto her back I begin to play with her limbs whenever I feel any holding patterns. At the end I remember sitting there with my hands on her right arm for absolutely *ages*.

Just the two of us, Mavis and I.

Very peaceful.

About three hundred years later I slowly withdraw my hands and say:

"So Mavis, when you are ready just bring yourself back to lying on the Massage table, here at number twenty-seven Clare Road in sunny old Halifax, will you? Perhaps open your eyes when you are ready?"

There is no response.

I hear the clock ticking and the whirr of the fan heater but nothing at all from Mavis except her breathing. Eyes closed tight.

Then her body shivers.

And again.

A shiver goes right the way down her body. I watch, fascinated.

Another shiver; only this time it is followed by another and then she starts to tremble all over. Her jaw looks clamped tight, so I say,

"Mavis, just soften up your jaw would you? Let the trembling out - if you are happy to, that is. You can stop it anytime you want but this is perfectly normal; all part of the medicine, so to speak."

There are pauses but the trembling increases in intensity until her whole body is literally shaking. I can even feel the table legs vibrating against my knees. Not sure what this is about really, but I have learned to trust these healing releases *whatever form they take*.

"Well done, Mavis. Just let the shaking come all the way out of you, nothing to be frightened of. Perfectly natural way for your body to let go."

After a while it becomes clear to me that this is not going to subside for a while. I can hear voices from downstairs and I realise it is Richard letting in my next client.

I look at the clock and realise we have run over.

Time to move her on

"Ok Mavis, so when you're ready just get yourself dressed. Keep the shaking though, let it carry on. Dress shakily - no extra charge, okay?"

She smiles at that.

When I come back into the cave she is sitting there in

the wicker chair, dressed and shaking from head to toe -
looks like an attack of the shivers but Mavis is smiling and
looking at me, eyes bright.

"How are you doing with all this releasing, then?" I
ask.

"It's a bit ruddy weird" she replies and then looks at me
out of the side of her eyes, "You ain't gonna lock me up,
are you?"

"Good Lord, no!" I laugh.

*If I locked you up Mavis, I'd have to put the whole of
Halifax in an asylum, including myself, I'm afraid*

I'm getting anxious about the time and my next client
waiting.

"You okay to drive home yet, Mavis?" I ask.

She looks at me quizzically.

Then she starts laughing.

Yes.

Ridiculous question, really. Absolutely ridiculous.

You *goon*, Grant.

"Probably not, by the look of things, eh?" I continue,
"Probably end up in Alaska actually, by the look of you." We
both laugh.

Then I pause to try and work out what to do.

"I tell you what: why not make yourself a cup of tea
downstairs in the kitchen? Take your time, let yourself shake
as much as you need while I see my next client; only don't
leave until you're able to drive in a straight line, okay?"

"Okay" she laughs and makes her way shakily down the
stairs, with her left hand pressing firmly against the wall for
support as she goes.

Is our tough old Mavis reaching out for support?

When I finish my next session I go down to the kitchen
to see if Mavis is still there; and I see that she has washed
up her tea cup and left.

All trace of her is gone.

Just like Cinderella.

Didn't even leave a glass slipper, did she?

Chapter twenty

So when I turns up for me next session, I don't know what to think. I mean, I feels good but not as how I expected, like.

I feels loose but I feels different, too.

It's like me waters have changed, if that makes any sense? His lordship has touched on summat so deep inside me I feels like I've lost me balance somewhere; that I'm not quite myself anymore.

And I'm still wondering what are all these scripts he talks of? And how did he know to decide to spend all that time on just one ruddy arm? And how come just touching someone can cause them to feel so wobbly and strange?

Me head is burstin' with a million questions it is and I just wants some answers, you know?

So I asks him.

About the scripts, I mean.

He's wearing them funny Chinese style trousers today - the pyjama ones he wore at Burton Manor - and he sits on the edge of the Massage table and says that these here scripts is just ways that we lives our life but sometimes we needs to change them 'cos they don't work anymore, like me shoulder hurting all the time.

"How's that, then?" I ask him.

He tells me that these 'ere scripts are stories we makes up before we are five years old and that we forgets as how we ever wrote them.

"Some people write stories with happy endings, but most of us write *tragedies*." he says. "And then we go on to live out this tragedy just like our life is a play in three acts with the full story only really coming out in the final scene."

"You mean like that song in Fame?" I asks, "You know,

the one Olivia Newton-John sings: *Tra-ge-dy?"*

He looks at me blankly. It's obvious he doesn't know the film or the song, does he?

I do worry about this fella, I really do.

I think he should get out a bit more often and enjoy himself. I mean, everybody knows *Fame*.

He's looking completely lost now.

Better help him out

"But why would anyone want to write a bad story about their life, then?" I ask, thinking that most five year olds I know just love happy endings, they do...

"Well," he says, " The main thing to understand about life scripts is that we decide on them before we're fully *compos mentis*, so to speak."

He's starting to get very excited he is, like he could talk about this all day long.

"You see, we make decisions about life that are based on very limited information, and then we sort of write those decisions into a life story all for ourselves."

He gets up and walks over to the window and peeps out through the wooden slats.

What's he looking at?

"And the only stories that most five year olds hear are fairy stories, actually. Even today with all these horrid computer games, believe it or not. Before five years old, most parents are still reading their children fairy tales and nursery rhymes. So, if you scratch below the surface of someone's life story, I mean *really listen*, then what you often find is a fairy story, actually."

"But aren't they mostly happy endings, these fairy stories? You know, like living happily ever after?" I ask.

"Well, absolutely!"

Now he's really going, he is.

"That's why they look so *attractive* to us when we are little; and so we think 'that's my story! That's the one I want, that happy one right there will do me fine'. But when you think about it, Mavis, are they really all that happy?"

He turns to look at me, smiling. He looks like a professor

giving his favourite lecture.

He puts his hands behind his back and starts walking around the Massage table. I know I couldn't stop him if I tried now, so I just settles down to hear him out.

I'm quite enjoying this, me.

"Let's see, now..." he goes on, "Snow White spends her whole life fleeing from an evil witch who always seems to find her, doesn't she? Strange that. Dear old S.W. seems to have a bit of a sabotage going on, doesn't she? Keeps leaving clues all around the place and talking to dodgy old women with poisoned apples!"

He laughs and looks at me.

He carries on walking around; he's really going off on one, isn't he?

"Hardly a secure or fulfilling life, is it, eh? Always on the run... Bit of a fugitive actually, our sweet little Snow White, don't you think?" He stops over at the window and looks out again.

Now he's just talking to himself, isn't he?

"What about old Cinders then, Mavis? I mean take her story... Cinderella works the first part of her life away as a virtual slave forever waiting for someone to turn up and rescue her. You could call her the ultimate passive victim. Gambles her whole life away waiting around for someone else to come and do something about it; waits her whole life for a fairy godmother who may never turn up! And then, to cap it all, once everyone in the whole land knows the prince is searching for her, what does she do? Just sits there, hoping he will turn into some kind of brilliant detective and just happen to find her. Leave it all to someone else, why don't you, eh, Cinders?"

He steps away from the window and starts walking around the table again, hands behind his back, looking down at the floor.

The professor

"And what about Sleeping Beauty, Mavis? *She* sleeps her life away until everyone she knows is dead. You couldn't think of a less friendly or connected life... And Rapunzel? What about her? She is imprisoned for most of her life by a vicious old crone and then is directly responsible for the man she loves being blinded. She is your classic *femme fatale*. Want to hear any more, Mavis?"

"No! I gets yer point!" I say laughing; but he isn't even listening now, is he? He just carries straight on...

"Take Rumpelstilstkin. What a genius! He can turn straw into gold; I mean he's your archetypal inventor! And what does he do with this gift? Why, he gives away all his knowledge to help someone who is never going to honour her agreement and he dies frustrated and embittered... And what about the Ugly Duckling?"

He's getting louder now and starting to fling his arms out every so often. A bit scary, actually.

"I mean the poor little beautiful swan is a laughing stock for his whole life for being different and in truth is your classic scapegoat to all around him and so on and so forth..."

He looks up at me as if he suddenly remembers I'm here, like. Then he smiles at me and comes over and sits back down on the edge of the table.

He looks at me and says, quietly,

"Even the ones with happy endings have a bit of a twist to them don't they? I mean take the Ugly Duckling, for example: how well does the Ugly Duckling really get on with all those swans at the end of the story? Think about it. He's literally a 'duck out of water'. To them he's just an interloper, not one of the family at all."

Now this fella may be off his rocker, but he's got me riveted with this stuff, he has.

I can hardly breathe.

"So where does he go then, our Ugly Duckling?" He looks at me, "Where's home, so to speak?"

He gets up and starts walking again, not even bothering to wait for an answer...

"I mean, can he ever go back to his original 'Duck family', Mavis?" He says, looking over his shoulder at me.

I say nothing.

"No, Mavis! His is a *lonely* script."

He's standing in the far corner of the room over by the window. The light puts half of him in shadow. I'm getting goosebumps, I am.

He continues, "One where he lives out his life as an outcast. Never fitting in. Too much a duck for the swans and too much a swan for the ducks, sadly."

He pauses, dramatically.

"Personally, Mavis, I think he dies a sad and lonely death, wishing he'd stayed pretending to be a duck no matter how much fun everyone made of him, no matter how misunderstood. Sad and lonely, see?"

He's looking out the window.

I'm dumbstruck, I am.

I ain't never thought of people living out their lives like a fairy tale. And there was me thinking that he was away with the fairies, like! Now I discover that we're all living in a fairy tale.

He crosses the room and sits down on the table again.

He's looking at me kindly, now.

Like he's giving me time to absorb all this, nodding and smiling like he can see me putting it together.

He's waiting for me questions.

But now I'm lost. I can't even remember why we're talking about all this...

So I asks him how this all fits in with me Massage like, and all the funny feelings I've been having since he messed around with me arm, 'cos I'm not quite making the connection, am I?

"Well, good question." He says, "Very good. Enormous question that, actually. Not sure I can answer that one in less than a couple of years, Mavis. But I'll have a go, shall I?"

I nod.

I hopes yer don't take more 'n' a few minutes 'cos I still wants me Massage, don't I?

He pauses and closes his eyes and takes a deep slow breath.

"The truth is, Mavis, that we spend the whole of our lives following our own particular script, like we are in a dream; a bit like *sleepwalkers*."

Then he gets up and goes over to look out the window

67

again and says,

"Until something or someone wakes us up from the dream."

He doesn't say anything else.

Just looks out the window. I'm not sure what to say.

What is he looking at?

So I coughs, politely, like.

"Then," he continues like he never stopped, "When we wake up from the dream, we have to start asking some very hard questions of ourselves, we do. Damned hard, actually."

He looks down at his hands and goes all silent. He looks sad, he does.

The room goes very quiet.

He sniffs, pulls himself up, turns to me and says,

"And so Massage can do that." He looks at me and his eyes is full they are, you know, like he's been crying.

But *bright*. He comes back, sits on the table and says,

"It can put us in touch with parts of ourselves we thought were not even there, at least not while we were *sleepwalking*."

I gets the feeling he's talking about something personal, but I don't really know what he's on about, do I?

But he's off again:

"Through Massage we can rediscover all of ourselves, not just the parts that fit into a script we wrote before we were five years old. Good Massage touches all of us; our whole body: arms and legs, front and back. Not just bits of us. But it can also touch all of us, you know, body mind and soul. We remember parts of ourselves that our childish scripts left out. So after lots of Massage, one person may eventually start writing poetry. Another might change their job to something that has meaning for them. Another might set off on a mission that they realise is their true purpose in life... all because they reconnected with themselves. All through something as simple as Massage."

He pauses, like he's only just realised this for the first time. Then he says,

"Remarkable, really."

And he looks at me with them soft blue eyes of his, and he tells me that sometimes there is an emotional part to it as well, that our mind and our feelings can get all churned up in this process of waking up and changing.

"So it's not just all physical, like I were taught at me college, then?" I asks, knowing full well it ain't and wondering if he saw me tears last time.

And he asks me what I think?

And so I tries to evade his question by saying, "Well you're the ruddy expert aren't you?" laughing, like.

But he doesn't laugh, does he?

He says all serious, like, "Well no, I'm not, in fact."

Then he tells me that the only expert on me body and me life is meself. And he says all the Massage does is give me a chance to get to know meself better.

And I'm thinking, well, if I took me car into a garage and the mechanic says "Well, Mrs Poops obviously I'm the mechanic but you're the expert of your own particular car so you tell me how I should mend it", then I wouldn't never ruddy come back to *that* garage, would I?

But he must be reading me mind, mustn't he? 'Cos he just carries on talking and says how most people talk of their bodies like they are as simple as something mechanical, like a car which is just bits of dead metal stuck together.

And then he looks at me and says, "Don't you think us humans are a bit deeper and a bit more complex than that?"

Now I'm getting spooked.

How did he know that I were thinking about cars, like? But he's gotta point, ain't he?

So now I'm wondering what makes him so certain that this here arm is to do with me life and me feelings, I mean what does his lordship know about my life? I don't tell nobody about what goes on inside me head - I makes certain of that, don't I?

Except for me John, of course.

I tells everything to him and he never takes the piss about anything well, you know, *serious*.

So who the hell is his lordship to know that me shoulder and me arm ain't just the physical strain of lifting our Mickey all the time; just like them doctors said?

But just as I'm thinking this I starts filling up again, don't I? 'Cos I know there's more to it than that, really. And I know I'm just filling up, I am.

So I says, laughin', like,

"Oh ruddy hell look at me and we ain't even got started yet, have we?"

And I think he gets a bit embarrassed, the poor love, and so he says why don't we just get on with the Massage? So I nods me head.

'Cos I don't want him getting upset on my account, do I?

Chapter twenty-one

So now I'm lying on me back and he's well into the Massage, like.

And every so often he takes me arm or me leg and starts doing the same thing as last time - and he keeps saying stuff like, "That's it, now just let it go, Mavis. Give me all the weight of your leg" and then he says "Oops-a-daisy Mavis you just took it back."

Oops-a-daisy?

Sometimes I just don't know what planet his lordship's on, I really don't. I don't know about them fairy tales but who the hell goes round saying "Oops-a-daisy" nowadays?

And then I has an attack of the giggles, cos I starts imagining him in pantomime, all dressed up in a pink fairy costume with a little wand saying in a very *camp* voice "Oops-a-daisy, Mavis", and I tries me best to keep me face straight as I'm lying there on the table, you know?

I don't think he noticed me giggles like, and he's off again giving me a running commentary on how much I am holding on and how much I am letting go. And everytime he does this, well, he might as well be speaking ruddy Russian for all the sense I can make of it!

Shlobdovotsnik jernostky, Mavis

Well blinking *nervotsnik andonnovitch* back to you, mate! 'Cos I'm going ruddy cross-eyed trying to let go and it just sounds like you're speaking friggin' Russian to me:

Shlobdovotsnik jernostky, Mavis

After a while I think I gets so confused I just can't be bothered anymore and suddenly he says in English,

"That's it! *Well done*, Mavis."

And I smiles 'cos it were when I stopped trying to do it right that I let go completely.

And then I thinks, well if it were that ruddy easy, why

didn't you say so in the first place? And then I really begins to feel the difference between holding meself tight and just letting go.

It's like I has to let go of me breath and me whole body all at the same time if I wants to let go of the bit he's holding.

And he's mumbling Russian to me again, only now I just stops listening 'cos I can't be bothered anymore and all I'm thinking of is me breathing and getting all the air outta me lungs before I breathes in - just like he told me to - and to hell with everything else.

And suddenly it happens again...

I'm being tossed all over Halifax, aren't I?

Only this time it's different: like I ain't so scared of being thrown around and falling and then being caught. And you know what? I realise it's actually fun to be scared - well a bit, like - and we go so ruddy high we're right above the clouds and Halifax is a tiny dot below us and he looks at me with a really mischievous glint in his blue eyes as if to say "you ready?"

And I just know this is going to be scary but like a crazy cow I don't care, do I? So I reaches out me hand, and I nods me head thinking: in for a friggin' penny, in for a pound...

And he just yanks me arm straight down, faster and faster like he's going to pull me arm out its ruddy socket and there's this deafening rush of wind and it's like me eardrum's burst and we're screaming down so fast towards the ground and he's not even looking at me, he's just looking straight ahead, determined; like he's some ruddy nemesis what's come to bury me deep in the ground. Now I'm scared

I really am

And I turns to him to say, can we stop now? And I were only kidding, like! But he ain't listening and the ground's rushing up towards us so fast...

And just when we shoulda hit the ground he suddenly stops dead in mid air, like, and swings me like a ruddy boomerang and the g-force pushes me teeth into the back of me neck and he just hurls me skimming along inches above the ground so fast I can't even breathe

And I'm skimming at a hundred miles an hour heading straight towards this ruddy great cliff wall of granite...

Chapter twenty-two

Well it weren't granite, were it?

It were just a thick grey mist and now I'm flying right through it. And I start to feel myself slowing down and then me feet lands on this cold wet grass and I'm standing in this quadrangle and it's very old and very quiet...

As I looks around, I suddenly recognise it

I'm standing in the quad of the convent I used to visit what's right next to where I did me teacher training all them years ago. It's lovely and old and there's cloisters running all around the grass, and I'm standing in the middle, next to a lovely oak tree, I am

But everything's grey and I feels cold

Actually I feel alone - like I'm the last ruddy person left alive on the planet. And there's this terrible emptiness inside of me like a deep ache. It's like there's a big hole in the middle of me and I'm thinking why does me chest suddenly hurt so much?

And then I remembers

This is the day right at the end of me teacher training; I've just qualified as a teacher and it's me graduation day, it is

I must be twenty-two

It weren't easy were it?

Getting me qualification as a teacher, I mean. What with all them posh grammar school girls and them grammar school lecturers; 'cos I were the first student what came to their college from a comprehensive, weren't I?

And I used to have stand-up rows with all of them 'cos they was always knocking comprehensives, they were. And I just had to put 'em right and say as how they didn't know their lugholes from their arseholes, didn't I?

Well someone had to tell 'em, didn't they?

They was so *superior* about themselves, and yet I would never have got to college without that comprehensive school, I wouldn't.

And I learned so much while I was there.

I learned stuff that everyone should have a chance to learn about. And them lecturers really helped me to think things out fer meself, like; they even seemed to enjoy the stand-up rows with me, they did.

And I learned about so much, you know?

I learned about literature and dance and all the Arts and I even learned about hiking in the mountains when I did the Geography section and it were all stuff you would never get time to learn and talk about if yer just has to go straight into a job at sixteen and stay living with yer family, like.

But them *lah-dee-dah* grammar school girls and lecturers was always talking them comprehensives down, they was.

Just because they was new.

I mean, where's the learning in that, then?

And there I am, alone in the convent when all the other students is celebrating and happy like, you know, with all their friends and family. Nobody in me family came up for my graduation or even said "Well done, Mavis".

It would have been nice if someone had said "Well done, girl - for slogging your little heart out and doing all that work."

Never said nothing, though, did they?

Not like what I did when our girls graduated - made a right fuss of them we did! Got all dolled up and then we took 'em out for a real posh meal.

Aw, that were good, it were.

Them all grown up in their gowns and still smiling like they was me little babies. I was so proud I reckon me face were split from ear to ear with smiling, you know?

I do miss 'em now, though.

Don't get me wrong, I wouldn't want them hanging around me into their forties or anything sad like that. I mean, I reckon if yer does your job right, then they flies the coup good and proper and only comes back ter let you know how good their life is - or when there's a disaster.

But you know what?

Sometimes I find meself secretly wishing as how they would have a few more disasters - just so I could help 'em out more, you know? 'Cos I misses those days when we was all together.

I really do.

So now I'm standing here in the quad, 'cos I don't fit in with all them other girls and their posh families what have come up to celebrate. They all looks like it were so ruddy normal you know, to celebrate together but I don't know what to do with myself

'Cos nobody's celebrating with me

So I've just wandered off into the convent for some privacy, ' cos I don't really fit in do I?

And now me chest really hurts, it does

I didn't know a space in yer body could hurt like that. It ain't a sharp pain but an empty ache, you know, one that pulls everything in like it's sucking me downwards and inwards and I realise it's a feeling that's always been there, it has

It's like a bruise

There's only ever been our John and me kids fer me.

You know?

And I really think they saved me life 'cos home's the only place where I felt safe. It were the only place where what I did mattered to anyone or that anyone said anything happy, like. And you know what? Out there in the big world everything felt so, well, horrible. And what could I do to make any kind of a difference, anyway?

When I finished college and started teaching it were like everything just *hurt* too much. All the kids and their pain and the stuff they had to put up with in their homes; and all the teachers could think about was their free periods and sniping at each other and picking on them poor kids.

But here in me house with my family, here I could really make a difference, couldn't I? I ain't no politician what could change the world, but right here with me little family I could make it a good world, you know?

I suppose home was the one place where it were all down to me, wasn't it? Whatever was going on in the world, here in me home I could make the sun shine, couldn't I?

So I did, didn't I?

I gave up me job and looked after our John and the babies.

And that were good, it were.

Then suddenly, there's this voice saying as how it's "time to end the session" and to open me eyes gently but I don't wanna open them, do I?

'Cos I'm still three hundred miles away in a convent

And then I starts to feel like I'm shivering with the cold and his lordship puts more thick towels on top of me but it don't make any difference, does it?

The trembling gets bigger and bigger till the whole of me body is shaking and I'm thinking what the ruddy hell is going on here then?

You're losing yer marbles, Mavis Brown, that's what's going on.

If I'm not careful they'll be coming in their white coats and wheeling me away, won't they?

And I'm shaking so much now, I can even hear the Massage table rattling and I'm trying to stop it I am, honest.

But I can't.

And now I'm really scared, I can tell you.

Then I hears his lordship's soft voice telling me ter keep breathing and as how this is all "very normal" and that I'm doing so well and not to fight it but to let the shaking all come out, like.

"Better out than in, Mavis" is what he says.

And that's exactly what it feels like. It's like the shaking is deep in me bones and now it's coming out.

And then I can feel the tears burning down the sides of me face and I just hopes he can't see them, but of course he ruddy well can because he's right next to me, isn't he?

And the shaking just goes on and on and I think I might

as well open me eyes, mightn't I?

And he's just sitting there at the side of the table smiling at me with his happy baby-face smile as if this was the most normal thing in the world to do and so I says summat daft about putting me in a straight jacket and he just laughs, you know?

That laugh of his is like a waterfall; all cleansing.

And then he just walks out telling me ter get dressed when I'm ready, even though I'm still shaking me ruddy guts out!

And then the penny drops and I realise...

All this stuff *really is* normal for him, isn't it?

The mad bugger.

I reckon I'm Shaking Stevens and his whole ruddy band all rolled up into one, me

Chapter twenty-three

Anyways, after I'm dressed I'm still shaking and I'm thinking, so basically I haven't got arms anymore, have I?

'Cos what I have got is a pair o' ruddy snakes that just keeps shakin' and moving all on their own and I still don't know what the ruddy hell is going on; so I asks him don't I? And he says not to worry but to just let meself "unwind".

So now I'm a ruddy clock what's unwinding, is that it?

I'm not sure what the ruddy hell I am anymore, to be honest.

I mean one minute I'm a friggin' knitting pattern with a few loose stitches and the next I'm a contract like what you sells your ruddy house with and then I were a friggin' script what 's auditioning for a ruddy play and now I'm a clock what's unwinding and coming apart and I'm thinking:

What is he on, like?

And then he says he's got another client waiting and as how I should sit downstairs and only leave the centre when I feels ready to drive. I looks at me watch and I thinks everything really is unwinding - including me sanity, like - 'cos it's only a few minutes over the hour.

But I feels like I've been away for years, me...

So after making meself a nice cuppa tea I'm sitting downstairs in this kitchen and I'm looking out the window at the back of all them nice old Victorian buildings. And I'm thinking about when I was at college and as how I really was quite lonely there, you know?

Of course, I have to use both me hands to drink me tea, don't I, 'cos I'm still shaking all over. But I feels *good* despite all this shaking and I can't explain why.

It just does.

Feel good, I mean.

It's like what is happening were meant to happen. It's a feeling that comes from deep down like, you know, like it's just *right*.

So I wobbles back to me Mickey-mobile and makes me way back along the M62 not really knowing what to feel or think about all this Massage.

I rings him up a couple of days later just like he told me to - 'cos I does what I'm told as far as his lordship goes, don't I?

I mean if he can read me friggin' mind like that last time then there's no telling what he could do ter me, is there? Sometimes I can't work out whether he's just a stupid old toff or some mad crazy witch doctor.

I mean if he opened the door for me next session dressed in skins and feathers and skulls and chanting some crazy song I wouldn't even blink an eyelid, I wouldn't.

Honest.

Anyway, I tells him over the phone that I dunno what to do with me ruddy arms; I don't know whether to let them hang or fold 'em up against me chest, or what the ruddy hell to do with them, do I? And if I lets 'em hang, then I feels like a gorilla with them swinging all around the place! And then I tells him as how me head's just aching from all the ruddy questions that just keeps going through it, about all this releasing.

And he says to keep me head out of it and tell him what I can actually feel.

So I tells him as how I feels lighter and freer all over me body I does, like I bounces more when I walks, you know? He seems pleased with that he does, so I probably got that answer right, didn't I?

And I tells him about all the pain I had in me chest during the last Massage and he goes real quiet, like and then he just says, real gentle like,

"You're doing some *very deep work*, Mavis, so be good to yourself, okay?"

Like he really cares. And you know what?

I think he does.

'Course I didn't tell him about me stupid memory in that quadrangle, did I?

I mean, if I told him I were having flashbacks like that he'd probably call out the men in white, what with him being a qualified psycho-ruddy-summat-or-other so I'm keeping me trap shut and me head down, I am.

Anyway it's none of his ruddy business is it?

But that night I sat at our dining table and talked late into the night with me John, didn't I?

And I told him all about me graduation day at college and I had a little cry didn't I?

'Cos it were always so ruddy hard, not never fitting in nowhere, like. And I did really well to even get into that college and it were real hard for me doing all them assignments you know, what with having ter write all proper, like. I mean I know I didn't come top or nuffing but I felt like I had, didn't I?

Come top, I mean.

And I refused to let all those toffee-nosed buggers win. I mean, just because you can read and write clever stuff, doesn't mean you has to change the way yer talk, does it?

'Cos I likes the way I talk, I do.

It's how me family talk and all the people I grew up with talk. And why would I want to change that for a bunch of stuck up grammar school tossers who would probably slam the door in me face if I popped round just ter borrow some milk?

You know?

But it were still hard.

And this Massage seems to just open the floodgates from all those years ago and all the tears come pouring out.

And me John just held me, didn't he?

He just kept stroking me hair and calling me a daft old cow,

"Which is good" he says, smiling and kissing me softly on the head,

"'Cos I'm the friggin' milkman, ain't I?"

And I ain't gonna tell you what we did then, am I?

Chapter twenty-four

When Mavis arrives for her sixth session there is something, well, *dishevelled* about her.

I'm running late and still in session with another client; this time a psychotherapy client who couldn't be rushed. So I ask Mavis to wait for a short while downstairs and go back up to finish the session. This client then asks if she can sit and make some notes in the therapy room we are using before leaving. So I leave her up there and go and get Mavis.

When Mavis eventually walks into the cave she looks strangely *hesitant*.

A bit odd actually.

Before I can leave her to get undressed, she blocks my way and says:

"Now look here, I need ter know whats going on. I mean *really* going on. I never knew coming for a Massage would do all this, did I? Why am I feeling so ruddy strange all the time? Inside, I mean. And don't give me any more of that fairy tale stuff, neither. I just wants to know what all these changes are; 'cos I don't know if I'm coming or going, I don't."

She looks me straight in the eyes, hands on hips.

She is wearing trainers, jeans and a coarse brown fisherman's smock today. Her hair is distinctly uncombed and her eyes are glaring at me.

She looks *windswept*, she does.

Like she's just come back from a fishing trip, actually.

I sit down on the Massage table and take a slow breath. Important moment, this.

"Listen, Mavis, have a seat, will you?"

I get up again and and move the waiting towel off the wicker chair. She sits down, eyes still fixed on me. Clearly my script discussion with her hasn't helped her understand the shift she is feeling *inside*.

"I wish there were easy answers as to why all this happens... I really do."

I sigh.

Don't know where to begin.

Don't know where to end actually.

She waits. She's going nowhere until I explain.

We're like two boats stuck in the *doldrums*, Mavis and I.

Strangely, I hear the sound of sea gulls and look out the window.

It's a dull metallic day outside and the wooden blind makes everything in the room look like it's covered in a layer of brown dust.

Mavis' face looks *granular.*

Her eyes, however, are burning.

Well, here goes,

"Of course, we *could* sit down and theorise about all this for hours. Nothing I enjoy more, actually. But what happens to the Massage, then? It's gone, Mavis. Lost amongst all the words and all the talking."

She stares at me. Drinking in this information, she is.

They are an open people that live in this land. But do they trust me enough, yet?

"Thing is," I continue, "We can have a post-mortem if you like. Absolutely. But not now, okay?" Still looking at me, waiting for her explanations...

"It's really a question of *momentum*, see." I continue, "Could you perhaps trust me with this one, Mavis? I mean, you can ride a train without even knowing how the engine works and assume that it's all working, can't you? I mean, you trust the driver without even meeting him, don't you?"

She nods her head slowly.

"Thing is, we're actually on the train right now, see? Hurtling down the tracks, actually. Not a good time to get out the carriage, spanner in hand, and start taking everything apart to find out how it all works. Little bit windy at a hundred miles an hour, actually!"

She smiles.

"Is it possible for you to just enjoy the scenery for now, do you think, Mavis?"

The good stuff comes from much deeper down than the mind in my experience. It comes from deep inside the body and it is impossible to explain *beforehand*.

I look her in the eyes and smile at her, saying:

"After all, we know where the train is going, don't we? Loosening up this shoulder, eh? And you are doing splendidly, actually Mavis. Making real progress - right from that first session in Burton Manor you have been a model client, okay?"

Mavis accepts my words, nods her head and says,

"Okay," and then, "Fair 'nuff".

But what I am really feeling from her is anxiety.

Gone a little too fast, we have.

Once she is on the table I ask: "So Mavis, tell me: apart from all these questions running around inside your brain, is there anything you particularly want from the session today?"

"Not particularly... erm, not sure really".

Rather a confused and hesitant Mavis is what we have here, today.

Mavis is developing doubt, she is

First she discovers gravity and now she's discovering doubt.

"Perhaps I can help you out a bit, here? Got an idea, actually; like to hear it?"

Definitely time to slow the train down a bit so we can take the bends more safely. Mavis is scared, that's what she is.

"Go on then" she says.

"How about we have a little 'Massage holiday' today, Mavis? Just iron out the kinks, stretch the muscles and oil those joints. Nothing too heavy, nothing too complicated; keep it simple today, eh? Nice and physical; slow everything down a bit, what do you say to that?

"Yeah, that sounds great." Her voice brighter.

So that's what we do.

And this is another Mavis entirely, it is.

She is so soft during the Massage that she seems to drink in the touch like parched Earth. She lets out her breath *magnificently* all the way through the Massage and even makes some sounds as I work on her.

Murmurs and grunts.

There is such an exciting flow and dance to this session. I am thrilled by the sheer physicality of every second of it. I am in my element today, dancing wildly with Mavis in my dark cave.

One moment I am travelling down her back like a steamroller and the very next moment I have turned her over and the whole session is finished - in less than five seconds it seems.

Sad to end the session, I am.

And dripping with sweat, actually

Chapter twenty-five

Now I knows what it must feel like to go bungy jumping, I does.

I never have, mind.

But it must be like as how you knows yer don't have to do it and it scares the ruddy tits off you, but you still wants to do it and then it must be like, well, as you're falling through the air you has to trust this ruddy rope; 'cos that's all that's stopping you from certain death, ain't it? And then when you're okay at the end it must be such a ruddy great feeling.

Well I feels like I'm about to jump off the ruddy bungy crane as I stand outside his lordship's manse in Halifax for the next session, don't I?

I'm staring at this big blue door but what I really wants is to just drive home and tell me John I can't be doing with all this Massage stuff anymore. But I knows I would just come back, so why not get on with it and ring the bell, you silly old cow?

So I does.

Ring the bell, I mean.

Mr-ruddy-haw-haw won't never win no friggin' prizes for his bedside manner, will he?

He opens the door and without so much as an "Hello Mavis", tells me he's running late and to wait in the sitting room and then all I sees is his back as he runs up the stairs. And me mouth's wide open with a hundred ruddy questions and all I can think is, same ter you mate.

Nice seeing you, too!

But I don't walk out, do I?

I mean if he's as good with everyone else as he is with me then I ain't surprised he runs over, am I? I don't know how he even gets through one day with this stuff happening all over the place; whatever it's all about.

So I'm sitting here in the big training room downstairs, the one with all them cushions and them nice bay windows and I can just hear me John saying to me that if he's worth travelling all the way down the M62 to see, then maybe it's worth trusting what he says?

Like a bungy jumper has to trust the rope, you know?

Of course me John's right ain't he?

Now there's a man I would trust with me whole life... Well I have haven't I?

I mean, I married the fella!

When his lordship comes down to say he's ready and I go up the stairs into the room I'm wondering, what the ruddy hell has he done with his last client, you know?

'Cos I ain't never heard anyone come down them stairs, have I? I suppose I was hoping to get a glimpse of one of his other clients, nosy cow that I am.

But no one's come down the stairs have they?

So I'm peering gingerly round the door when I walks in just in case his lordship's forgot they're still lying there in the treatment room - well he looks like he's the absent minded sort, don't he? - but there's no one there!

I mean, what the ruddy hell has he done with them or did they just transfigure and ascend to heaven like the virgin ruddy Mary?

No wonder he's running over, I thinks to meself: transfigurations must take a little more time than your average one-hour Massage session, like.

Then he asks me to get meself undressed and on the table and starts to leave the room, and I just blurts out, bold as ruddy brass, like:

"Listen mate, before yer starts: how about telling me what's going on? Why am I feeling so ruddy rotten all the time and then so ruddy brilliant? How come me arms feel like they belongs to a ruddy gorilla and I don't have a clue where to put them and why do I keep crying and then bursting out laughing?"

That stops him, it does. He looks shocked at me outburst.

And I tells him how I was even watching *Chicken Run* the other night and I just couldn't stop crying with stupid ruddy laughter; and me John and our Mickey was just pissing themselves with laughter; not at the ruddy film, like, but from watching me split me ruddy sides every time one of those daft chickens said anything at all.

So what's going on, then?

I mean, what's that all about when it's at home, like?

And d'you know what his lordship tells me?

I mean he sits down all serious like and I thinks, great! I'm finally gonna get some answers to all me questions, like. And then he starts going on about climbing outta trains at a hundred miles an hour with a friggin' spanner! And I'm thinking, what is this fella on?

I mean is he taking drugs or summat?

And to cap it all, he really puts himself out don't he? He finishes off his train speech by saying as how I should stop worrying about all the "whys and wherefores" and to keep trusting me feelings for now.

And it must have took him all of 30 seconds to say that, didn't it?

Well thanks for your time, mate.

Sorry to bother yer, like.

And then he pronounces, all pompous like, that he thinks we should "slow things down a bit".

For no reason that I can think of.

So he starts Massaging me again, but it's like he's lost the plot ain't it? 'Cos I ain't never had a Massage like that from him before: it's like I'm being worked on by a ruddy whirlwind, I am.

He ain't never worked so fast on me before.

If this is "slowing things down a bit", thank goodness he didn't say "we should speed things up, Mavis" is all I can say, 'cos I barely had time to breathe, I did; it were like I were being Massaged by a whirling dervish, it were.

And then there's this strange smell, sweet but also thick and, well, like the smell of soil after rain; all damp and fresh

89

at the same time.

And one minute he's working through these lovely thick dark blue towels, and the next he's spreading oil all over me back and like, *steam-rollering* me into the table, and then the next minute he's covered me in towels again, and is rocking me from side ter ruddy side like I'm a friggin log and he's a lumberjack rolling me down the river turning me this way and then that way...

And then he goes and puts on this strange tribal music what has all these drums and people singing and shouting, like.

And it feels like I'm in a jungle with that crazy witch doctor I were talking about, and he's dancing around me and pummelling me to bits, you know?

And so here I am lying head down with me face looking to one side and I opens me eyes at one point and all I sees is his feet and them baggy trousers of his.

And the next second they just leaves the floor completely, don't they?

And now he's working on me back from the other side of the table, ain't he? And then his legs is back on this side again, and I thinks, ruddy hell!

He's jumping over the friggin' table, he is!

Today's another baggy trouser day, see.

I better watch out for that one next time, hadn't I? And then he's rolling down me back again and pushing all the ruddy air out me body like I'm a piece of dough and just as I fills me lungs again he's at it all over again, and I'm thinking, perhaps he's just doing this so I ain't got no chance to ask him any more questions, like.

I think I'll keep me trap shut next time.

And everything he does feels so deep; like he weighs twice as much as before. And a part of me body's shouting "Oy! You'll break me ruddy bones you will", but another part of me's going *this is ruddy fantastic, mate*. 'Cos it never hurts, not even with all this pressure. And a couple o' times, when I really am just about to shout out in pain like, he moves on somewhere else.

Like he just knew.

And I think the smell is making me hallucinate or summat, 'cos I keep thinking I really am in this jungle, you know? And then I feels a part of me crying out for some more pressure right on that spot there...

And that's exactly what he does next.

And I'm thinking, he really can read me ruddy mind, can't he? And on he goes never pausing for a second, like, and I has to keep breathing 'cos basically,

it's either that or die.

And he's pushing all the air out of me and it feels like he's pushing everything else out of me as well, you know, all me crap, like.

And now I really am hallucinating, 'cos I'm just blowing it all out like smoke, I am.

It's like I can see all the crap o' me whole life leaving me in the breath. So basically, I'm breathing out this black disgusting smoke and it's all just disappearing into them trees over there in the jungle...

At the end, after the storm has passed, I'm just lying here in heaven, I am. He's put some different music on now and there's this woman what sings like an angel, doesn't she?

Beautiful it is

When I opens me eyes I can't move, can I?

I'm probably dead, I thinks to meself.

I ain't never felt so still in me whole life. It's like the centre of me is so still I dursn't even breathe for fear of disturbing it. Then there's a knock on the door and he says to let him know when I'm all dressed and I think, how the ruddy hell can I get dressed?

'Cos nothing on Earth is gonna make me break this stillness.

Then, a couple of hundred years later, he knocks on the door again and asks if I'm alright and I says "Yeah".

Of course I'm alright.

I ruddy well died and went to heaven didn't I?

But slowly I starts to move and as I gets dressed I suddenly feels sad - 'cos I knows I'm already losing that still feeling and you know what?

I feels like I knows what it must be like if you're an angel for three thousand years and then you gets told you has to come back and be an ordinary human being again, you know, what worries about the price of marmite and paying the mortgage and how bad yer joints is aching when you wakes up in the morning.

And I feels so *sad*.

Like I just lost the most precious thing on the whole planet and I can't even remember what it was...

And I finds meself sobbing at the utter beauty and loss of it.

Daft cow that I am.

But you know what?

It doesn't all go away.

I feels this stillness all through the next couple of weeks, I do. Like nothing could upset me and everything was just perfect, even when there were problems with our Mickey's social workers. And normally they just drive me to understanding homicide, don't they?

But I'm just *serene*, I am.

And me John keeps asking "Are you okay?" all the time which is funny 'cos I really am okay, ain't I?

Only I ain't never realised it before, have I?

Chapter twenty-six

At the end of the session Mavis takes absolutely ages to get off the table and as I stand outside the door I am sure I can hear her crying, quietly.

So after a couple of gentle knocks on the door I decide to leave her and eat my sandwiches for lunch downstairs in the kitchen.

It's obviously my day for running late, isn't it? In between bites I keep checking at the bottom of the stairs to see if she's opened the door; her signal that she is dressed and I can enter the room.

Not yet, though.

When she does open the door and I finally get into the room, her eyes are red but there is a *softness* to her face. She seems to be okay with her tears.

As I walk into the room I am struck by something *palpable;* a translucent wall that is like a soft skin and I shiver as I walk through it. I can smell the rich sweet frankincense oil I used today, but it is more than that.

The *silence* in the room stops me dead.

I breathe.

Listen, Grant
Listen to that silence

There is a white light around the room that makes the blue whale pictures look grey and the Massage table look pale. She seems more than okay, actually, does Mavis. She is standing by the wicker chair next to the blinds and she is shimmering.

Her skin has light shining out of it.

Something has happened.

I am not sure quite what to say. But that's the point really, isn't it?

There isn't anything to say.

You could fill a whole book trying to write about moments like this, you could. But the simple truth is that there isn't anything to say.

It just is

Chapter twenty-seven

So here I am, standing outside his lordship's great big ruddy sandstone building on a sunny, crisp November morning.

And yer know what?
I ain't scared at all, this time.
I just floats in, don't I? And he asks what I wants from the session, like. And I smiles serenely and says I wants more of the same please and he raises his eyebrows and asks,

"Same as what, Mavis; if it's not too much trouble for you to tell me, perhaps?"

But his eyes is laughing and I think he's taking the piss of himself and all his posh talk so I says I wants more of that stillness from last time, please? But then he goes all serious, you know, and says,

"Only something deep in your body can really decide on feeling something special like that, at the end of a session, Mavis."

And I'm thinking, so why the ruddy hell are you asking me what I wants at all, then?

But I'm too happy to argue with his lah-dee-dah-ship today and he goes and does a very similar Massage to last time like he's pressing all the air out of me again and I'm doing this breathing thing, just like he told me, and I'm breathing out smoke again, like.

And I'm lying here on this beautiful comfy table covered in them thick blue towels while his lordship does his whirling dervish number again, only today he's not going quite so ruddy fast, thank goodness.

Mind you it's still ruddy deep, like.

And he's wearing them ordinary black flared trousers and a black adidas vest, so it obviously ain't a Chinese-trouser day nor a baggy-trouser day for that matter, is it?

Today's an adidas day.

That rhymes with Lah-dee-d*arse* I thinks to myself, wickedly. So does that mean it's an ah-di-d*arse* day for his Lah-dee-d*arse*-ship? And now I'm giggling to meself but he don't notice does he?

Sometimes, I don't think he's even on the same planet as the rest of us. Either that or he's just too busy leaping over tables, probably. But don't get me wrong, I'm loving every second of this and I'm drinking in every second of his touch, I am...

Then he turns me over and starts pushing and pulling at me legs really slow and gentle - but it's like me whole body is moving; so how's he doing that, then?

'Cos he's only got me feet and then suddenly...

I'm falling off a cliff, me

I'm tumbling over and over like I've gone and fallen off this really high cliff and then I lands on a ledge with me feet and it's okay for a bit but I'm trying to keep me balance on this tiny ledge and then me weight takes me over and I'm falling again until I hits another ledge and then I falls off that one all over again and I'm tumbling from ledge to ledge and I'm thinking, ruddy hell, what's going on here then?

And then there ain't no more ledges, is there?

I'm just falling down and down through the air like this cliff were hundreds of miles tall and I can't hardly see the ground below 'cos it's so far away...

And I've been falling for ruddy ever down and down and then I looks to me side and there's his friggin' lordship falling down next to me!

And he's grinning like a Cheshire cat, he is

He's just lying on his back with his hands under his head and his feet crossed like he's on a beach and saying ter me, "look Mavis, no hands!" and he laughs at his own joke and pulls a silly ruddy face at me and I just has to start laughing don't I?

'Cos he's such a ruddy kid, he is

And that just encourages him, like

So then he starts showing off and doing all sorts of

somersaults and I'm thinking, Mavis, you finally cracked you have 'cos you're falling to your death here, and all you can do is laugh at a friggin' madman what's pulling faces at you and sticking his tongue out; anyone would think he's trying to distract you, wouldn't they?

Which is good, really

'Cos the next thing I know, there's this hard concrete surface what suddenly comes up and cracks me in the back of me head at a hundred ruddy miles an hour

Chapter twenty-eight

And I can see me schoolbag flying through the air spewing out me beautiful colour pens all over Scotland Road

And I thinks, ooh look! They're drawing a rainbow in the air all on their own

And there's this squealing of car brakes and this ruddy great car tyre's burning smoke and I can see the zig zag patterns 'cos I'm staring up at them just inches from me nose and the burnt smell is horrible, like

There's cars stopped all around me and all these people what is rushing up to me, but all I can see is this red bus disappearing and not one of them buggers on the bus is looking back, and how the ruddy hell am I gonna get to school on time, now?

I'm thirteen and I'm standing on the back platform of a bus in the busy rush hour traffic only I'm not standing am I? I'm ruddy well falling backwards off the end of it...

I can't stop meself, see?

I'm reaching out as I fall back trying to catch the pole but it's too far away and me fingernails is just scratching this man's mackintosh but there's nowt to friggin' well get hold of and then I'm falling backwards...

I were relieved, like, 'cos I'd only just caught the bus, hadn't I? I'd have been late for school if I missed it. And then, as we're going along I steps back to give some space to this woman what wants to get off at the next stop only there's no ruddy platform to step back onto, is there?

That's why I'm falling backwards into three lanes of busy rush hour traffic on Scotland Road, it is

Then there's this man what's looking down at me and asking me how many fingers he's got - and all I can think is, why can't he count his own ruddy fingers?

And I hears this other man saying as how he nearly had a heart attack 'cos he thought he'd run over this "ruddy kinder" and did he see how ruddy close to her little ruddy head the ruddy car stopped and as how he needs a ruddy stiff drink right away and off he goes

And I thinks, well thanks very much, mate

Don't mind me too much, will yer?

And then I thinks the whole world's gone mad, you know? 'Cos now there's this lunatic woman what's wearing a daft hat with funny plants sticking out of it and she's picking up all me pens off the road and showing them to me and wittering away like a constipated parrot asking stupid questions about "didn't I have a pink pen as well as a purple one, dear? 'Cos the pink pens is best for a nice girl, aren't they?"

She did, honest

And then two men is helping me onto the pavement and I'm smiling and telling them I'm just fine which I'm ruddy well not 'cos me head hurts rotten and I feels sick and like I've been given the whack all up and down me back a million times, I do

And now I'm walking to school all on me own, holding me head and trying not to cry and there's this headache what runs all down the back of me neck into me shoulders and it's killing me, it is

I even got a detention for being late, didn't I?

And I ain't never told nobody about this before.

Not even me John.

I suppose I just hadn't really thought much on it, like. But now it feels like I came two inches from ruddy dying didn't I?

And I never said nuffing

Then I hears his lordship's posh voice saying, "Okay Mavis, take your time to get off the table." Only me legs start this trembling again, don't they? And it travels up me whole body and I thinks, here we ruddy well go again.

And he stays in the room and tells me to keep me jaw soft and open and not to try and stop the shaking and of course that just brings the trembling on faster, don't it?

So now me whole body's doing a friggin' St Vitus's dance, you know? And so I opens one eye and squints at him and says outta the side of me mouth,

"I couldn't ruddy well stop this if I tried, like."

And he laughs and says "Well done Mavis, good show."

And I thinks, well jolly hockey sticks to you too mate; I mean I'm glad you're happy with it, I really am but I still haven't got a ruddy clue what's going on here, have I?

And he's just smiling and saying as how it's normal to release like this and you know what I'm thinking?

If this is normal mate then we're in real trouble, you and me

Chapter twenty-nine

When I'm dressed, I'm still shaking all over and he says, "Would you like me to tell you what I think is going on, Mavis?"

Hale-ruddy-loo-yah

He's finally going to tell me what's going on, he is!

And then he says it feels to him like all the energy in me body just wants to be free and that sometimes he thinks me body's gonna tap dance its way off the table all the way to China with me legs all moving and me whole body shaking and dancing, like.

And when he says this I starts to fill up again, don't I? He asks if I'm okay to drive home and I nods me head, and then he says is there anything I wants to tell him, before I leave?

And I shakes me head and then he says all gentle, like,

"Perhaps you might just want to think about putting your clothes on again, Mavis."

And I says, "What?"

And he's smiling and comes over and real tender like, he just pulls at the label in front of me neck and I've only gone and put me shirt on back to ruddy front and inside out, haven't I?

And I starts laughing and so does he.

And we just stands there looking at each other and laughing.

And I know I'm laughing, like, but really a part of me's crying at all the ruddy stupidity and all the lost dreams in the world.

You know?

And I'm laughing about just how funny a back-to-front shirt can be when yer just came two inches from being run over and losing your life on Scotland Road...

And I ain't got a friggin' clue as to what his lordship's laughing at, have I? Except I know he's completely bonkers anyway, and that just sets me off even more.

I bet he likes Chicken Run, too, the soft bugger

You know, after everyone had told me I were stupid to want to dance about a hundred thousand times I did finally give up on me dream. But then, when I was training to be a teacher I thought, maybe I could do some dance now?

So I did.

But I never really *danced*, did I?

It were all about teaching the kids to dance which was great, like, 'cos I love kids but it ain't the same thing as doing it yourself, is it?

Anyway, I rings his lordship up a couple of days later and I says all cheeky like,

"I've worked it out, I have. You ain't never gonna answer any of me questions, even if I asks them, are you?"

And he laughs and says, "Well, actually no, Mavis. Probably not at all."

And I starts laughing all over again and there we is, just laughing down the phone together.

And then I realises I'm ruddy crying at the same time and this just makes me laugh even more, I mean how ruddy ridiculous am I?

Only he's not laughing now, is he?

He's just listening and then he says all quiet, like,

"Well done. I'm so very proud of you, Mavis."

And that just sets me off crying worse, don't it?

But I can hear him doing that loud breathing thing of his, like, and I know he's with me at the other end and it's like I can feel this connection with him, like he just knows how I am without me saying hardly nothing, and so I says, you know, between sobs, like,

"Is this really ruddy normal?"

And he just says, all serious like, "If you really think that what we're doing is normal, Mavis, then there's even less hope for you than I thought..."

And that just sets us both off laughing again, don't it?

Anyway, after I calms down he says, all posh and serious again,

"So Mavis, could you tell me what it is that you have actually been *experiencing,* if you would be so kind?"

So I knows we're back down to business, don't I?

And I tells his lordship as how I could feel me body trembling all over for the first couple of days and how it ain't really stopped yet, like it just goes inside for a bit and then it comes out again, you know?

And I can even hear it in me voice 'cos it sounds like I'm friggin' ninety three, it does.

For all the shaking, like.

Then I tells him as how I've got this rotten cough and cold now, which ain't like me at all 'cos I'm never ill, am I? And I told him as how I never knew so much snot could come out of one person!

'Course I didn't tell him that underneath the lousy feeling of the cold there was this feeling of deep joy like I ain't never felt before, and even when I'm blowing me nose and running with snot, I still has this feeling of *lightness,* don't I?

Nor did I tell him as how I'm getting this feeling that I am beginning to understand this whole body-mind thing.

'Cos it just feels like I'm snotting out all the rubbish from me life and that every time I blows me nose it's like all the rotten bits of me life are just pouring out, making me lighter and lighter, you know?

And so he just says well done and that he'll see me in a couple of weeks...

I ain't never ill, me

Chapter thirty

Mavis turns up for her seventh session looking happier than I have ever seen her.

She is full of energy is our Mavis. She says she wants "the same again, please", like she's ordering from a menu. She is wearing a smooth cream suit with a soft floral shirt and a lovely pair of pearl earrings. She puts up her hand as she walks through the door and laughs,

"I'm not all dressed up smart for you, like, so don't worry... It's just that I gotta go to a ruddy tribunal after, with all them sodding social work tossers; the ones that think they can tell me as how to look after me Mickey."

Verbose, is our Mavis today

I ask if it is an important meeting and she replies,

"Nargh... It's another new fella, and they always feels like they has to try and justify their useless ruddy jobs when they're new, you know? So they holds a case meeting and gives me some useless advice 'cos they've been on the case for, what, all of three months? And what the ruddy hell would I do without their advice, like? I mean I've only been looking after the fella for twenty years and I ain't never once managed to break his legs have I, so what do I know about anything?"

She's grinning widely as she says this.

There is a new flow and energy to her today and she asks for a session full of deep Massage with lots of energy and movement. It's only when I have turned her over and am working on her feet that I realise I have moved all her arms and legs today without the slightest resistance.

Well done, old girl

I'm gently pushing and pulling her leg by holding her foot whilst I perch on the table, sitting on my right leg. I do this very slowly and I can see her whole body moving, even her nose. She seems to be deeply affected by this movement and I don't want to move on. So we just stay there, Mavis and I, with me gently pulling and pushing her whole body up and down the table here in my little cave in Halifax.

I feel like I could stay here forever.

I look around the room and take a nice deep breath. Today the whales are looking happy and the room is suffused with a soft golden glow.

I really could stop here forever...

And I get the feeling that all this Massage is Mavis' get out of prison card, so to speak.

This is her body's bid for freedom after years of imprisonment.

Her solid and square body actually feels to me like the body of a dancer, a being of air, who has been trapped all her life in clay but is now attempting to dance her way to freedom. Her body doesn't stay still during the treatment like other clients, you see.

She is always shifting and moving like she is uncomfortable but I think it is because there is just too much energy inside her. She keeps moving to find freedom.

It's her escape from Alcatraz

After I have finished, she starts trembling and shaking again only this time she opens one eye and makes a joke about it. When she is dressed, I explain to her about my feeling that her body wants to dance and her eyes fill up again. So I ask her if she wants to talk about what is going on inside her?

But she just shakes her head.

Which is fine by me
Private, see?

When she rings up a few days later, it is clear how much she is de-toxing and what a great client she is turning into. Again, I remember us having quite a lot of laughter at how little I am letting her actually *theorise* about all this.

Keep the train moving, Mavis, that's the thing.

There is living life and then there is analysing life.

I cast my vote for the living bit and I think our Mavis is very much a 'liver', too.

There is such a lot of living inside her.
That's it, I smile to myself.
Of course...

She's my very own 'Liver' bird - flown all the way over from Liverpool and the Mersey to visit me, hasn't she?

Chapter thirty-one

When Mavis comes back for her eighth session she looks *clear*. All flushed out and *detoxified* from the cold, I suppose.

Her skin glows and her eyes shine brightly, they do. Halfway during the Massage I turn her over so she is lying on her back. I lift her feet an inch off the table and start gently swaying her legs. Only this time her legs are resisting me when I move them.

Strange.

"I say, Mavis, can you feel a bit of the old 'arm thing' going on here, perhaps? Here with the legs, that is?"

There is a pause.

"Yeah... I think so... kinda..." she says.

"Mmmm... Well, Ah! That's it - just there!" I start to explore the tension with my movements... "What do you say to us spending a bit of time on this: do you feel up to a bit more *exploring* today then, Mavis?"

I have already started, actually... know her body's answer already.

"Yeah, why not?" she replies.

Why not?

Well I can think of many reasons why not, actually. After all, why not keep everything just the same; maintain the status quo, eh? The trouble is, Mavis, the price tag is something we only discover afterwards, I'm afraid.

And there is always a price to pay, believe me Mavis.

Not really fair, this one.

It's like we go into this sweet shop and just grab as many of the goodies as we want; things like health or energy or whatever good things we get from these Massage treatments, and then we just walk away from the shop, arms full. No complaints from the shop keeper, no complaints at all.

Smiling at us is this shop keeper.

Free gifts all round. Help yourself, be my guest

But then, two years later the little fat shop owner turns up and knocks on the door, asking for payment. Looks like a civil servant he does now, wearing a suit and mopping his sweaty brow with a handkerchief.

"How much do you want me to pay?" you ask.

"Well now, let me see..."

He pushes his glasses back up his nose and looks at his clipboard with those piggy little eyes of his... "Ah yes, here it is... Your job, please, yes that's the price for this particular change."

Or another time he says,

"I will have to take your house, I'm afraid." All smiles. Another time he just says,

"Your friends. Says here I must take all your friends away from you." Has the smile of an undertaker, this fellow. Wears a bowler hat, too.

Another time he says,

"I'm terribly sorry but this change you made was rather an expensive one, I'm afraid. So I'm here to take away your wife and all her family." And then just to *rub it in*, "You know, the ones you have known and loved for the last twenty-eight years of your life?"

Smirking, he adds, "That alright with you, then?"

If you're really unlucky, then he just puts his clipboard away back in his briefcase, looks up at you and says, all business like as he walks past you into your house,

"All of it, I'm afraid. It says on my sheet that I'll have to take the whole lot together, I'm afraid. The job, the house, the friends, your wife and all her family."

Which is what the price tag was for me actually, Mavis

Why not?

A thousand reasons why not, actually. Only I don't know what price you will have to pay for this change, Mavis, so how can we even begin to talk about it?

All I know is this: if any of us knew the actual cost of healing I'm not sure a single human being would ever make any damn change at all.

It's just the house rules, this delayed price thing.

Nothing I can do about it, Mavis, nothing I can say to really warn you, I'm afraid.

It's the Ugly Duckling thing again, see?

The dear old Duck found his freedom and learned to fly, but what price did he have to pay?

Found his freedom and lost everything he knew, he did.

"Ah, there you are, Mavis... Just there! Can you feel it; how you're holding your leg up, actually? Any chance you could let me have the weight of your leg again - resurrect our dear old friend, Sir Isaac, perhaps? Breathe a little, Mavis? That's the ticket... there we go... got it! Well done old girl, Sir Isaac's back in business, now... Jolly good show."

She laughs at my foolish banter and on we go for quite a while. I let her know whenever she takes control and whenever she lets go.

Again and again.

A hard worker is our Mavis.

Normally impatient, there is something about doing this work that gives me all the patience in the world. But only here, nowhere else - as anyone who knows me will tell you.

I mean, ask me to fix a toilet seat and if I can't do it in ten seconds you will find me sitting on the bathroom floor whining about the impossibility of life and how nothing ever works and it's *just not fair*. But give me a human leg to move and I am happy to sit here all day.

It's like I am picking a lock, see?

And every little tension and even the tiniest little movement holds the promise of real treasure. So I sit here like a man obsessed and the truth is, I'm just happy to learn a little more about locks every day.

I feel no rush.

No *pressure*, see?

Gripping under her heels I make slow random movements. Mavis starts to let me 'float' her legs through the air more and more.

Then the legs suddenly go very heavy and I can really feel their weight and I know Mavis has made it.

She has let go.

She is all unwound.

So I lay her feet gently on the table and leave the room...

The lock is sprung

Chapter thirty-two

It's friggin' freezing today and it's pissing down with rain, so I'm standing with me nose pressed up close to this here blue door.

There's a tiny little ledge over the door and I'm trying to stand under it and not get completely soaked, ain't I? Only when his lordship opens the door I almost falls inside like a wet rat, don't I?

Which sets us both off laughing, don't it?

When I'm on the table and all warm and dry in these lovely thick clean towels - he does keep his room nice and warm, doesn't he? Anyways, when I'm lying on the table all nice and warm, he asks me what I wants from the session, like?

And I tells his lordship as how I'm feeling lighter than I ever felt before in me life; now the snot's finally stopped pouring out, like! And so he says what does I actually want from *this* session?

"Apart from all the shaking and the snotting?" I asks?

And he laughs at that and then says quietly, all serious like,

"Well, Mavis, thing is this: if you never say what you want, then how on Earth are you ever going to get it?"

Which makes sense to me, it does.

So I stops wittering on and I breathes, and I has a think about that. And when I thinks about it, the thing I most wants is freedom like, so I says, a bit nervous and quiet like,

"I wants to feel freedom in me body, I do."

He must think me crackers.

But he don't, does he?

'Cos he just starts pressing down on me body all over

and saying the word "freedom" over and over like a ruddy madman! Actually it felt like a kinda prayer, you know?

But it really felt strange, like he's putting the ruddy word into me body like when you makes currant bread and presses the currants into the dough and he's just pressing the word into me like he believes me and would help me do whatever I wants and that sets me off 'cos I can't remember anyone except me John believing in me like that, I can't.

Lucky I'm lying face down so he can't see what a soppy old cow I am.

Anyway I carries on breathing like he tells me to and for some reason he spends ages on me legs like he did with me arms, kind of moving them and letting them fall and I finds it really hard to tell when I'm holding on or when I'm letting go and he keeps talking away saying stuff like "There you go, you've taken it back again" and he keeps asking me can I give it back to him?

And he's speaking ruddy Russian again, ain't he?

Only I ain't listening this time, am I?

'Cos his voice becomes like a murmur and after a while I can't be bothered to work it out, can I? And then the next thing I know,

I goes all dizzy...

And I'm spinning around and around like I'm the friggin' blades of an helicopter

And his hands are spinning me round and he's taking me high over the top of Halifax again and we're inside the clouds and he's tilting me this way and that and I'm just feeling sick I am, all queasy like

And then he flips me upside down and he's just grinning at me from above and spinning me with his hands and I'm just keeping me eyes fixed on his blue eyes every time I come round so I don't get any sicker and he looks at me as if to say, "are you ready, Mavis?"

And I says "Yes"

Mad cow that I am

And he starts spinning me faster an' faster and then

he pushes me down towards the ground and it's like he's spinning me so fast that when we hits the ground we just spins deeper and deeper into the earth with mud flying everywhere and we're digging a tunnel and we're going down so ruddy deep and fast and then it's like we suddenly breaks through the roof of this cave and I'm falling into darkness...

And I'm walking home from the shops carrying two heavy bags of food

But something's scaring me

I'm only seven years old and there's this man on a bike what's holding out this paper bag of sticky black and white humbugs and saying to have one and I knows I shouldn't but they does look so nice and he's saying as how he only lives around the corner and he could put them bags on his handle-bars and wouldn't I like to have a little rest before going home what with these heavy bags an' all?

And then he says as how he's got this lovely little daughter who's at home now with her mum and as how they could probably help me carry them shopping bags home and that his daughter was about the same age as me and we would probably get on really well but something's really wrong, it is

He smells bad; all sickly, like

And he keeps shoving this paper bag with them sweets at me and I'm smiling and saying "No thanks, Mister, I gotta rush home for me tea" 'cos this man feels like inside he's made of tar or summat and not solid at all and if I gets too close I'll drown in all this tar and what he's made of is scary and I knows I mustn't let him see I'm scared, don't I?

So I keeps smiling and then I suddenly turns and runs down this alleyway which is a short cut into me garden and he stops his bike at the end and he keeps looking at me and I'm thinking, please God don't let him come down here after me! And I'm trying to run but it's hard with these heavy bags and I can't drop 'em 'cos me Mam will kill me so I goes as fast as I can, with them bags bashing against me legs, like

And then me back gate's locked

So I bang on it real hard and I looks back and he's still there watching me and I starts kicking the gate and shouting, "Let us in, our Mam!" real loud like, and me Da' opens the gate 'cos he's taken the day off and he's gardening, ain't he?

And I just rushes past him and puts the bags in the kitchen and goes straight up to me room and I can't hardly breathe and I just stands there in me room looking out the window to see if he's followed me round to the front, like

But I can't see him...

And there's his lordship's voice telling me to get off the table and get dressed and later on, as I'm driving home me legs start shaking so much I has to stop at Birch services 'cos I'm worried I can't drive, you know?

And I'm sitting in me van, and the shaking goes all over me body and I just starts filling up again 'cos I ain't never felt this sick feeling before, and it's like, well, *dread*.

That's what it is.

I'm feeling scared right through me body, I am.

Dread

I can't get rid of it and the shaking's deep inside me belly. So I just closes me eyes and does that deep breathing thing he showed me and then I hears his ruddy lordship's voice inside me head telling me that what I'm feeling is all part of the releasing and anyways I shouldn't worry, should I? 'Cos he's already reserved a place for me in the local looney bin, hasn't he?

And I'm smiling now and I opens me eyes and looks at all them cars whizzing past on the motorway and I wonders,

Why do we all rush about so much?

'Cos now I'm feeling better, me. And soon I'm okay to drive home 'cos I'm getting used to me insides shaking and wobbling, ain't I? And every time I goes over a bump in the road it sets them off even more...

Old wobbly-guts is driving down the M62 back to Liverpool, ain't she?

Chapter thirty-three

So when I turns up for me next session, I says to him, "Can I just have a *normal* session, like?"

And he raises an eyebrow and pulls a melodramatic hurt face, saying, "All my sessions are normal, don't you know?"

And I has to laugh at how he plays the fool, but then he looks at me all serious like, and asks what does I mean?

"Well," I says, "What about just doing a Massage without stopping and playing around with me arms and legs, like?" 'Cos between you and me, if I gets much more of this shaking and snot pouring outta me I think I'm gonna go crackers, ain't I?

But he looks at me all serious like, and says he can't do that 'cos it would mean him pretending he wasn't seeing what he was seeing; like he was pretending to be blind.

"It would be like driving down a deserted road, Mavis" he says, "Late at night. And then coming across a car accident with someone lying on the road, hurt. I mean I can't just drive past; the very least I have to do is to stop and see if I can help, isn't it? Can't just ignore it, can I?"

I don't know what he's on about, do I? So I says,

"Well of course if I were the body on the road, I would be glad of you stopping, wouldn't I?"

And then he just looks straight into me eyes with those deep blue eyes of his and says,

"Mavis, that's exactly what you are."

And that shuts me up good and proper doesn't it?

But you know what I really thinks?

I think his lah-dee-dah-ship don't like anyone telling him what to do, for all his ruddy 'contracts'.

Anyways I think he got me point, 'cos instead of

messing with me arms or legs, guess what he goes and does? Well, he only goes through the whole session like a ruddy whirlwind again without stopping once, doesn't he? It just felt incredible like me whole body was humming and tingling at the end.

And no shaking afterwards, neither!

And his lordship says as how I really went with the Massage that time and it just made me think, well thanks very much, mate...

So what do you think I were doing all the other ruddy times, then?

But I feels too good to feel bad.

And this time I don't think me Mickey-mobile even touches the road as I fly down the M62 and I'm thinking as how I've got this one cracked for sure - just another couple of sessions and I won't have to be making this journey anymore 'cos me shoulders are feeling great and I feels younger and lighter than I ever felt in me whole life and I can't stop grinning about nuffing at all, can I?

So that woman you can see driving down the motorway in that big van with a grin right across her face...

That's me, that is

Chapter thirty-four

So now I've got this 'flu bug haven't I?

And it's just before me next session and I'm so rough I can't go, can I? I don't mean any old 'flu neither. I mean the mother of all frigging 'flu's, I do.

In fact I ain't never felt this ill since I was little and had jaundice. So I rings him up and tells him I caught this bug and all Mr-ruddy-pomposity-himself can say is that he don't believe we catches bugs, actually. So I just says,

"Look here mate, you wanna come over here if yer don't believe in bugs, 'cos a bug is definitely what I have caught."

And anyway, what the ruddy hell is he doing to me 'cos I don't never catch bugs, do I?

And he just starts laughing down the phone and says that this is just me body taking charge and getting rid of stuff like with the snot, and not to worry 'cos it happens all the time. And I'm sitting here at the bottom of me stairs in me dressing gown with me body aching all over thinking, that's nice, ain't it? 'Cos I has to pay for the treatment, even if I don't turn up.

And so now I'm thinking what a great ruddy business idea that is then: to have people pay you to make them all sick and then charge them when they can't turn up so's you gets a paid holiday!

I'm probably just a mug, me.

Then again, I suppose he could have seen someone else in that time, couldn't he? When yer thinks about it, he shouldn't really lose money just because I'm ill, should he? Deep down I just feels miffed that I can't see him today. I think I must really value them sessions in Halifax, don't you?

Not that I can even get out the door, mind. I can barely

crawl back up the stairs to me bed, I can.
    I don't ever get ill, me.

    Never

Chapter thirty-five

Mavis cancels today because she has 'flu.

I have to smile: 'flu?
Not a hope, I'm afraid.
You are letting go from a deeper and deeper level, Mavis. Now it's the resident viruses that have been sitting around in your body for all these years, being ejected.
When she turns up a fortnight later, Mavis looks tired and reports having 'no energy'.
So we have a very quiet session.

I simply move around her body gently pressing and releasing through the towel.
No oils at all.
Slow *repletion* work. She likes this session and looks much more solid and 'here' at the end.

Very quiet we are today, Mavis and I

Chapter thirty-six

So when I sees him a couple of weeks after me 'flu I still feels a bit under the weather, don't I?

And he goes and does this session where his hands just stay still and he gently presses in and out and I feel all this warmth, and before I've even closed me eyes, the session's over and he's asking me to get off the table!

I has to check me watch 'cos I can't believe the session lasted more than five minutes, but he's actually gone longer than the last time, ain't he?

So what's that all about when it's at home, then?

Anyway, when I walks around the table afterwards I feels like I've been to the petrol station and got meself all filled up, like.

How can this be called the same as the last session? I mean, every ruddy treatment is so different from the last, like he can play a million different pieces of music and he just picks out the right one for me each time, he does.

The clever bugger.

Don't get me wrong.

I ain't jumping around with loads of energy or nothing, but I feels more solid and strong and as how I got this sort of slow but deep energy running through me. It's very different from the fast buzzy exciting kind of energy I felt before, like the other stuff was all fizzy and fun like; only this is like a deep underground river, it is.

Aw, listen to me like I'm a friggin' connoisseur now; talking like I knows anything about all this 'energy stuff'!

His lordship says it's about giving me body a chance to recover and build up its own energy quietly. He says the body can find its own energy naturally if we gives it half a chance without us forcing it or pushing it around and that just makes a lotta sense, don't it?

And as I drives home in me Mickey-mobile along the M62, I think as how I really have become a bit of a connoisseur, haven't I? I mean look how much I've changed and how I ain't at all nervous about having his lordship massage me and how it feels the most normal thing in the world now, don't it?

And just at this moment there's this programme on the radio saying, you know, what would you do if you were the prime minister, like? And I'm smiling to meself thinking as how I know exactly what I'd do.

I'd make sure every single man woman and child got a Massage every week, I would

But it ain't all easy.

I mean it changes you, it does.

It's like watching a black and white telly and then suddenly getting a colour TV set and everything is different even though you're watching the same programmes; which is great for all the travel and nature documentaries, which I loves, but it ain't so good for all the gory horror stuff like; 'cos that's in full colour too, ain't it?

And that's how I feels I've gone; from living in a black and white world, to seeing all the ruddy colours of the rainbow. And now me life swings from feeling much happier than I used to be, ter feeling a hundred times worse than before. When I feels sad and down I feels much more vulnerable and kind of exposed than I ever did, you know?

I think I used to just *tough it all out* and get on with the job and don't get me wrong, I can still do that, but now I can feel when I'm all wobbly inside, and I can feel if I'm scared and it's strange 'cos I feels like people can see right through me, you know? Like I can't hide anywhere, and I used to think that if I just kept meself quiet, I was invisible.

But that's just daft isn't it?

'Cos people can always see you, can't they?

So really, there's no point pretending 'cos folk always know you're there, anyway. And you know what I thinks?

I think I were really just hiding from meself.

And now I can feel me big bum on the seat while I'm driving, can't I? And I knows that I'm quiet and thoughtful, right now.

And I can enjoy that.

I can just feel me energy sitting happy in me belly, like a reservoir and I never used to feel any of this before, did I?

It's like I'm just me

So here I am and this is Mavis, like.

I'm driving down the M62 in me Mickey-mobile and feeling me bum and thinking these thoughts and this is just how I am. So I looks in the mirror and smiles at meself and I says, "Ello Mavis."

You're all right, you are

Chapter thirty-seven

I feels like ruddy superwoman when I drives down the M62 for me next session, don't I?

And I'm thinking that this will probably be me last session and as how I'll miss his lordship but I feels so great; I mean this is me eleventh session and I can't really justify all the time and expense, can I? Anyway, he does this weekend thing called *Body Awareness* which I've booked on, so it's not like I won't see the old bugger again, is it?

I feels like me body's done all the letting go it needs to, and although I still can't figure out what to do with me arms and me walking never feels the same two days in a row, I *am* getting used to feeling everything being so different now.

And instead of only noticing me body when it hurts like, I'm noticing it all the time now; even when it feels nice. Which is kinda sad when you stop and think about it, ain't it? That I only used to notice me poor old body when it was screaming and not when it were purring like a pussy cat, I mean.

And as for staying quiet, well I can't hardly keep me trap shut now, can I?

I keep putting me hands over me mouth and thinking "I never said that, I never!" And the funny thing is everyone keeps laughing or else they stops and actually take notice like as if I'm talking some ruddy sense, you know?

Which I'm not am I, 'cos I'm such a daft old cow. But it's nice when people wants to hear what I has to say and I even went and gave a talk at me old aromatherapy school - me, Mavis Brown - giving a ruddy talk!

But you know what?

I really enjoyed it and I even made them laugh when I told 'em how ruddy useless I were when I started learning

123

Massage and as how I found it hard to even know where the friggin' spine were on me first practical, you know, what bit were bone and what bit were the ruddy back muscle, like, and as how at first I just thought an *erector spinae* muscle were something rude that only men could have, you know?

Mavis Brown, you never just said that, did you?

Anyway when his lordship asks me what I wants from the Massage I says (all expert like) could he just do a bit more work on me shoulder blades please, in case there is anything left to unwind, like?

See, now I knows what I am, don't I?

I'm a clock, see.

So I tells his lordship that I doubt there is, see - anything to unwind, I mean - me being such an expert of course, but just you know, to be sure there ain't anymore of them holding patterns lurking around to jump out and ambush me in the future; seeing as it's gonna be me last session.

Not that I've told his lordship that yet, have I?

Anyways, maybe he thought I was getting too big for me boots or summat 'cos that next session were the biggest ruddy session of me life, I can tell you! I shoulda known, 'cos he was wearing them baggy trousers of his.

And they always means trouble, don't they?

So here I am again, lying on me back in this little room at the top of the stairs, doing all that special breathing like what he asks me to do. And instead of working on me shoulder like I asked, his lordship's holding me ruddy foot up in the air and I'm thinking, what's that gotta do with me shoulder, then?

Does he ever listen to anything I say?

And then I starts to tremble and shake and I just thinks, oh no, not again you stupid ruddy cow. And he keeps asking me ter give him me foot and what have I done with our friend Mr. Newton, like?

And I'm thinking why can't we leave that poor old sod, Isaac Newton, to rest in peace? And then he's saying as how I'm pushing me foot up against him, and then he says not to press me foot down now 'cos he's trying to move it up, and I wish he would make up his ruddy mind!

And he's making them daft jokes all the time, like promising not to walk off with me foot, if I gives it to him.

Hah-ruddy-hah

And I just wanna say get your own friggin' foot ter play with, why don't you? And you know what?

I really wants to just kick him, I do.

'Cos I feels like I'm sweating ruddy blood down here at the other end of the table and he's just messing about like, and then I just kicks me foot down hard against the table in exasperation 'cos I don't wanna be doing all this trembling and shaking and holding stuff anymore, do I?

And it feels real good!

Summat releases an electric current right through me whole body like, and he just says,

"Ah that's it, Mavis, just do that again if you would be so kind". Like he were asking me to pass the salt at some posh dinner party, you know?

So I just kicks me other foot down on the table, trying to stop all this ruddy shaking. And I presses me heel down as hard as I ruddy can onto the table, and it sends another electric current right up me body. So I does it again, only now there's lots of explosions going on up and down me body like I'm a friggin' fireworks display, or summat.

Mavis ruddy goose green, that's what I am

And now there's this line of pain running straight from me feet right up into me shoulder blades, like a knife cutting up through me body like, and ruddy hell *does it hurt*. And how the ruddy hell did he know that me feet were connected to me friggin' shoulders like that?

The clever sod

And me fists are clenching tight now, and me breath is coming out real loud and I can hear him saying some rubbish down at the end of the table, but I ain't here anymore, am I?

Cos I'm just pressing down hard with me feet through all the pain 'cos it feels good as well, don't it? And then I suddenly stops pressing, and it's like I just catapulted off the ruddy table...

And I'm flying through the wall out across Halifax and I'm turning over and over...

I'm flying past all the traffic on the big motorway bridge and across all them moors and I'm just tumbling over and over; head over heels and I look to me side and there's his lordship right next to me all serene like, grinning his ruddy head off sitting in some yoga position

And he's saying "Here we go again, Mavis, old girl, just 'let go' and enjoy the ride"

Hey, less of the "old" if you don't mind!

And I would enjoy it a lot more if you could help me to stop turning over an over like I'm a ruddy pancake

But just like a fella he don't do nothing, does he? He just laughs and we're going so ruddy fast and I'm facing backwards, aren't I? And I'm trying to get me head facing forwards so I can see where we're going

So basically, I thinks to meself, I'm trying to look backwards to see forwards, like

When suddenly...

I smashes right through this brick wall at about a hundred miles an hour

Chapter thirty-eight

And I'm lying on me back on the kitchen floor with me fists clenched

And I'm opening me mouth to scream but nothing's coming out, is it? It's like someone switched off the volume and I'm just opening and closing me mouth but I can't breathe and I can't make any noise, neither

I'm two years old and me Mam's standing over me like a ruddy giant looking so angry and holding an empty bucket high above me head and there's still a few drops of water coming out of it. The rest of the water is on the floor all around me, swilling over the black and white lino like a pond and some's still streaming off me face and me clothes

'Cos she's just poured the whole ruddy bucket over me, hasn't she? She's screaming at me to "ruddy well shut up!" and as how "You'll be the ruddy death of me, you will"

And I can't even breathe 'cos nothing's coming in or outta me mouth, is it? And she's saying as how, "I'll ruddy well swing for you, one of these days" what with all me noise and while she's going on like this, I'm lying on the floor opening and closing me mouth like I'm a ruddy goldfish and she ain't even noticing that I'm like dying for lack of breath here, and nothing's coming into me lungs, is it?

And then the breath suddenly comes into me, only it's like I'm breathing through all these rubber flaps all hitting against each other hard when I breathes in, which I'm doing in little bits each bit jerking me chest up

And now she's telling me to stop making such a ruddy fuss and shouting about all the trouble I causes her and I can feel me whole body is like a frozen stone with this bit of air fighting its way in and then getting stuck inside and not coming out and then another bit wanting to come in but there's no room 'cos the last bit hasn't come out yet, has it?

And I can't feel or say nothing, 'cos all I'm trying to do is to breathe, like. And I don't know why she's just standing there screaming at me when I can't ruddy breathe...

'Course it were the family joke, weren't it?

How our Mavis had such a screaming tantrum on the kitchen floor when she were little that our Mam had to pour a bucket of cold water over her "to calm her down, like" and so I learnt to laugh at it like everyone else, didn't I?

But I ain't ruddy laughing lying here on the floor now, am I?

And all I can think of is how I ain't never gonna say nothing never again, am I? Nor am I ever gonna be able to breathe 'cos these rubber flaps is stopping me breath come through except in little bits and even then it's all noisy and shaky, like

So basically I'm dying then, ain't I?

And then I feels his lordship quietly slide his hand under me back so it's right near me shoulder blade and I feels his other hand touching lightly on me chest; even though I'm ruddy miles away and half a century ago lying on a floor in Liverpool...

And it feels real nice and warm and he's talking ruddy Russian again, isn't he?

Shlobdovotsnik jernostky, Mavis

Only now I understands it 'cos he's telling me that he's right here and it's okay and not to panic, like. And suddenly I ain't alone on that floor in the kitchen anymore. And so I says back to him in Russian, like,

Nervotsnik andonnovitch, Grant

Which is me saying, can you get me outta here?

And he understands me perfectly 'cos he just picks me up all gentle and tender like, as if I were his very own little babushka, and he carries me out of that horrible kitchen.

And we flies out of the house above Liverpool and back across all them moors...

And all the time he's speaking in that Russian only now I suddenly knows what he's been saying all along

He's been saying all soft and gentle like, that I don't need to worry about anything any more and how beautiful and clever I am and as how everything is just how it's meant to be, like. And he's saying as how I were born to dance and I have more dancing in me than all the ballerinas of the ruddy Bolshoi Theatre put together, I have

That's what he's been saying all along

And the tears are pouring down me face and he's still talking Russian and saying as how the breathing will come all in its own time and I ain't never to worry about breathing again 'cos we don't need it much anyhow

And then he says as how it's a "vastly over-rated commodity", all this breathing stuff, and he's saying it in his posh 'look-what-a-fool-I-am' voice and I has to laugh again at him, I does

You know what? I think's he's just about the daftest ruddy fella I ever met, what with all his stupid ruddy fairy tale ideas and his contracts and lost stitches and clocks what's all unwound, you know?

But I think that's when I realises just how much I loves the bugger, and how does he know all this stuff anyway?

And I can feel me legs shaking again, but it's like they're a hundred ruddy miles away on some table in Halifax and I'm just floating across them moors with his lordship and now he's telling me in Russian to keep me chin soft and open like, and I'm thinking how d'you do that, then?

'Cos I could crack a ruddy nut with this chin of mine

Chapter thirty-nine

And then we're back, ain't we?

And I'm on the Massage table with me legs shaking and me chin trembling, and the tears are running down the sides of me head. And I wants to turn me head to the right for some reason; but I can't, can I?

But he must have seen me try, 'cos he changes his hands so one is under me neck and he gently moves me head over to the right like I'm trying to look over me shoulder.

And he does this real slow and suddenly I feels this red hot pain right deep in me shoulder blade right where his hand is and he says ever so gently like, to sink into this place with him and it's like we're off again...

We're dropping down a ruddy hole and I thinks oh ruddy hell not again, ain't we done enough for one day?

It's like his wooden stool is falling through a hole in the floor now and he's dragging me down with him - you know, head first, like I were diving into the water backwards - and I'm looking down over me forehead at him and saying with me eyes, does we really have to do this?

But we're already falling down so fast and everything is rushing past us in a blur so I just locks onto his eyes, don't I?

And despite we're falling down so fast, he just looks all calm and serene and he says,

"One more time does for all, Mavis, okay?"

And I says, "Is it gonna hurt, like?"

And he just looks at me with these sad blue eyes of his that seem to come out of forever, they do

So I knows it will hurt, don't I?

"Let's finish the job then, shall we?" I says, doing me best to sound brave and he just looks at me, he does. And

you know what?
He's crying, ain't he?

And I still haven't ruddy breathed yet, have I?
And we're dropping down so ruddy fast and then there's this roaring sound and all of a sudden we falls crashing onto this rock. And when we gets up, we're standing right in the middle of this volcano full of molten lava all around us, heaving and boiling and he's still holding onto me, only now he's standing right behind me

And he's shouting into me ears 'cos the roaring noise of the volcano is deafening and he's saying, "Don't be scared, Mavis" like he's letting me know that he's right here with me and I'm thinking,

Me, scared? Why the ruddy hell should I be scared? You've only brought me into the middle of a friggin' volcano, mate!

And then he shouts over all the noise,
"Hold on, Mavis!"

And I thinks to meself, all this time he's been telling me to ruddy let go; and now he wants me to hold on

Typical fella

So I reaches over me shoulder and holds on to his hand, don't I?

And then I feels him press even harder into me shoulder blade and everything starts to explode all around us and we're just in the middle of this erupting volcano and it's like I suddenly realise that this volcano is me and it's all of me what is breaking apart and it really ruddy hurts, I can tell you

'Cos basically I'm losing bits of meself and I can hear all these voices like me Dad shouting at me and me teachers screaming at me and me Mam telling me as how she'll hang for me, and like all the ruddy scenes of me life is exploding outta me and there ain't gonna be nothing left of me soon, is there?

But where his hands are, right here on me shoulder blades, is all I am now. And I'm squeezing his hand so ruddy tight, I can tell yer, 'cos basically the rest of me is disintegratin', ain't it?

131

And suddenly it feels like I ain't ruddy breathed for years, not never; and that's because there's this hot bubble burning right inside me chest and then just when I thinks I'm gonna die from the pain inside me chest I'm not in the volcano anymore, am I?

'Cos I'm lying here all in bits on the Massage table, in Halifax, with this hot bubble in the middle of me chest and I realise I can't ruddy breathe 'cos there's so much of this hot stuff inside me, that there ain't no room for any air to come in, is there?

And I'm doing me best not to let it out and I'm just holding on tight to everything and his lordship says quietly,

"It's okay Mavis. Just let it out. That's it, right now. Go on. It's okay..."

Like he ruddy knows anyway, and so I lets it out and this enormous burp comes out! And it's real loud and long and it smells like sulphur don't it, you know, like bad eggs?

And I covers me mouth but he just takes me hand away from me mouth so gently, like, as if to say I don't have to shut me mouth ever again, and you know what?

I don't think I will.

And another thing: I can breathe, I can.

And ruddy marvellous, it is too. And then another burp comes out and he says,

"Well done, Mavis" and then another and another and now I'm burping for friggin' England, ain't I?

I couldn't stop it if I tried, could I? And he doesn't laugh once does he? He just keeps saying all serious, like,

"Well done, Mavis" after each one and his hand gently pushes me shoulder blade each time I wants to burp and it helps the burp come up, and after each burp I can breathe like there's a new space for the air to get in, like. And then the burping gets so big and loud I just has to sit up, so he holds the towels around me all gentlemanly, like.

So here I am, sitting naked on a Massage table in the middle of ruddy Halifax, at 11.30 on a Wednesday morning.

I'm covered in towels and burping away and his lordship is patting me on the back like I'm his very own baby, saying, "Well done" to me each time I burps; and I feels such a fool.

But I can't stop it, can I?

Nor does I want to stop it, neither.

'Cos each time I burps, it's like I'm finding space I never knew I had; like I been carrying all this hot air around inside me chest for a hundred ruddy years; so no wonder it ruddy smells, you know?

And each burp is like a blocked up drain that is finally getting unblocked, so everything can flow again.

I can't remember what we said at the end, but I remembers us having a giggle about the smell and as how that made me feel okay again, what with him telling me to go ahead and burp all week long!

And I looks up at him and says,

"So you think I could stop if I wanted to?"

And we looks at each other, and you know what? The thing I most like about his lordship is that he just knows when to say nowt, he does. And that's exactly what we does.

We says nowt.

We just looks at each other, smiling like. And you know what?

I think I just got reborn, didn't I?

Chapter forty

Mavis arrives for her eleventh session positively *brimming* with energy.

It's jolly good to see her so alive and happy after the exhaustion of the last session. She looks, well *younger*.

Very much a new model, this Mavis.

When I ask her what she wants from this week's session, she asks if I wouldn't mind giving her shoulder a bit of a going over; give it the all clear, perhaps?

No problem there, old girl

So during the first part of the session I prod and I probe, I jiggle and I poke all around her shoulder and find... well, nothing particularly. So I move on to the rest of her body thinking 'business as normal', so to speak.

When I turn her over she starts to tremble, she does. And then she kicks her foot down on the table as I'm trying to hold it. I can't quite get the measure of it, actually.

Then I realise that she is *pushing me away*. The feeling is most definitely that she is pushing me away. Feels like she's picking a fight with me, is our Mavis. So I carry on breathing and let her body do whatever it wants.

Clearly something is happening: she keeps pressing each foot down against the table one after the other very slowly, very deliberately.

That's it!

She is kicking her heels down onto the table in slow motion. This movement feels like a slow motion *tantrum*. Our dear old Mavis is having a tantrum, she is. Not sure quite what to do, so I just hang around the feet, saying:

"That's the spirit, Mavis, keep pressing down and don't forget to breathe. Jolly good."

The next thing is, she goes completely *limp*.

I'm not sure what is going on at all here, so I go round to her head to see if she is breathing. But there is no movement at all in her chest.

Now I know she has been breathing fairly deeply for the last few minutes, so I tell myself not to worry. Sometimes clients get over-oxygenated during a Massage, and they can go for quite a while without breathing at all.

So I'm kneeling beside her head with my hand on her shoulder.

And I wait.

We stay here like this for what seems like ages.

Just as I am about to panic and begin administering the last rites of holy Cardio-Pulmonary Resuscitation, Mavis takes a small breath.

Then another.

And now I have this overwhelming feeling that I want to work on her shoulder blade again, so I slide one hand between the towel and her back until my palm is cupping the back of her right shoulder blade (palm up, as it were, trapped against the table by her back) and my other hand is gently resting on top of her chest, palm down.

I close my eyes and sink into my *unwinding* mode, which means setting up a slow and gentle undulation between my two hands. It's just the same if you hold a balloon full of water between your hands and you squash it with one hand and feel the movement of the water against the other hand. I imagine a lot of swirling movements between my hands and do my best to just follow and flow with these tissue movements - imagined or not.

And before I know it...

We're sinking down deep
Straight into the place of swirling currents again
And we're being flung all over the place but I'm holding on to Mavis tight, I am
Don't worry, old girl, everything's going to be all right...
But when the currents stop, Mavis is just limp this time
There's no life in her at all. I'm holding an empty shell; just

135

a place where she used to live

And I'm all alone down here in the deep; holding the dead body of Mavis and all I can hear are the whales howling mournfully in the dark

And I'm feeling this sadness

Like an eternal sadness

It's a sadness that I meet again and again and I think it's the deepest pain in the world, it is. It's like this sadness has been going on since the world began...

And so here I am a hundred miles down in the ocean and I'm carrying the dead body of Mavis in my arms and the sadness wrenches at my chest and sucks the very life blood out of me

It drags me downwards into oblivion

And all I can do is scream silently in the deep

Scream at all the utter stupidity and evil in the world; scream for my pain; scream for dear old Mavis

Scream for us all, actually...

And suddenly she breathes.

We are back in the cave only now there is this bright and glaring light all around us. I feel the table vibrating so I open my eyes, unable to see anything for a moment because of the brightness. And then I can see Mavis' legs dancing on the table - doing an Irish jig, they are!

And she's smiling is our dear Mavis, while the tears roll down the sides of her face.

Mine too, actually.

I make some encouraging noises, more like grunts really, to cheer her on - let her know I am close by and *with* her.

With you all the way to the end, actually, Mavis

Then Mavis just reaches over with her hand and holds it out above her head palm up, and my hand is suddenly in hers.

The connection is made

Chapter forty-one

She grips tight, does our Mavis

And then she starts to burp.

Actually it's a bit more than a burp. It's like thunder rolling across the American plains, that's what it is. And it's the most glorious sound in the world... It's the sound of Mavis releasing, it is. The sound of her body beginning to dance again, actually.

And what a smell!

It's like walking into a hundred bad egg factories all at once - *very* bad, I'm afraid. These smells are coming from an ancient bog in Mavis' soul, they are.

Absolutely foul.

I encourage poor old Mavis as much as I can because she is clearly embarrassed, what with the burps and the dancing legs.

Then the burps start coming thick and fast until we have a veritable *burp-fest* on the go.

Huzzah! I want to shout.

I am suddenly elated by all this release and want to do something outrageous to celebrate, like run naked down Halifax High Street, jumping and shouting...

Instead, I just help Mavis into a sitting position before she drowns in her own burps; they all seem to come from this one spot, right here, in her shoulder blade.

Every time she squeezes my hand I press into it, the shoulder blade, and *hey presto*, she burps.

Well, she burps several times, in fact.

A serial burper is our Mavis

After she gets dressed she is sitting in the wicker chair by the blinds and still burping.

"Look here, Mavis, bit of advice, okay?"

She looks at me with a slightly worried expression on her face, wondering what I am going to say.

"Might be a good idea to cancel any dinner engagements, and hide in the cupboard under the stairs tonight - keep away from any *polite* society - okay?"

She laughs and looks relieved.

In between burps she asks,

"Is this ruddy normal" *burp* "like, or am I" *burp* "losing me head?"

"Well, Mavis, I did rather think we'd dealt with this whole *normal* thing a long time ago, hadn't we?" She looks up at me.

"I mean, I do think that all this sanity business is a bit *overrated*, don't you?" I look at her. She looks like she is about to say something.

Burp

Suddenly I feel angry.

"I mean, I tell you what, Mavis."

I walk over to the window.

"How about we both go out there and get sane, like the rest of humanity, eh?" I pause.

Then I turn to her and say,

"So we can destroy the most beautiful planet ever conceived, kill each other and starve anyone else that's left..."

Then I brighten up and say more loudly: "Why not, eh? Good plan! Let's go and get sane like the rest of them - you with me?"

Mavis is looking at me with her eyes wide open; like I am some kind of an alien.

Lighten up, Grant. You're scaring her

I hold out my hand melodramatically, inviting her to step out of the room with me,

"I mean come on, Mavis, let's do it right now, let's both jolly well go down to the town hall and apply for a sanity permit. Zombies of the world unite, and all that!"

Her face dissolves into laughter.

"Yeah all right," she laughs, holding up her hand in

submission, "I gets your point".
Burp

I sit back down on the table again, and look at her.

"Truth is, there's nothing *normal* about what we are doing at all, I'm afraid... But do me a favour, would you Mavis?"

"Yeah," *burp* "what's that?"

"Burp for Britain. Burp us a symphony for the insane, if you would please."

She laughs and we just lock eyes.

I see that light inside her again, the light that could make us all burn so bright...

Then, after a while, I say,

"Are you going to be okay to drive home, though?"

"Yeah" *burp* "I'll be just fine" *burp* "Don't you worry about me."

Buuuuuuuuuuuuuuuuuuuuuurp

"Ruddy hell!" she laughs.

So grinning and laughing, our blessed lady of the burps departs for the M62

Chapter forty-two

As I leaves his centre I'm rushing ter get to the privacy of me Mickey-mobile, ain't I?

So nobody hears me burping, like.

The ruddy noise of them!

Each time I opens me mouth, I don't know how long or how friggin' loud it's going to be. And some of them are really loud and really long.

Like they don't even belong to me, you know?

So here I am, burping all the way home on the M62 and I has to open the ruddy windows 'cos the stench of these burps is like nothing I ain't never smelled before, neither.

And I means *foul!*

And then, as if that weren't bad enough, I starts to fart for England as well, don't I? And I'm thinking you great fat smelly old cow!

How can one person hold so much ruddy air, I wonders? So I has to open the windows wider 'cos the smell is getting even worser and now there's a ruddy howling gale blowing through the van and it's all air, ain't it? I mean the wind's blowing through the van and all the wind's coming outta me, too.

And you know what?

I love it.

Cos I can breathe, me

It feels *so good* as it all comes out of me.

'Cos it leaves me feeling like I got more space in me body; like this is what all me tightness must 'ave been about, you know? It were just me air getting stuck inside me body, like as if I were a ruddy air mattress all pumped up tight.

And now I just feels relief as the air escapes and me

body finds all this new space again and it's ruddy great and I couldn't give a monkeys about the smell 'cos it's been inside me for years, hasn't it?

Better out than in, I reckon.

And I'm thinking as how maybe I ain't never breathed properly since that time on the kitchen floor; until his lordship told me as how to breathe out over and over, like. And maybe that's what set all this off in the first place - me.

Breathing out, you know?

The way he made me keep breathing out until all the air had gone outta me lungs...

How did he know?

Chapter forty-three

And now it's days later and I'm still burping throughout the day, but me farts have stopped.

Well mostly, anyways.

Me John's been taking the piss something rotten, hasn't he? He's been walkin' around the house with a clothes peg on his ruddy nose. He even tied a hanky over his face cowboy-style when he came to bed last night, the cheeky bugger.

"Enough's enough," I shout as I attacks him and we have one of our tickling fights under the duvet, with me screaming and laughin' me head off;

Only when he tickles me I starts farting again, don't I? And then we just both just collapses in tears of laughter, we does.

He must really love me, mustn't he?

And during the day he keeps taking the piss and calling everything *sulphurous,* so when he wants the salt he says,

"Pass the magnesium *sulphurous*, please"

Or, he asks me if I've heard the weather forecast for today? And I walks straight into it, don't I? 'Cos I replies all innocent like,

"No, is it bad?" and he says,

"Very bad. Apparently the satellite is picking up a strange build up of *sulphurous* cloud, over Liverpool." And when he answers the phone he looks at me, smiling, as he says,

"Hello, this is the *sulphurous* mining company speaking, how can I help you?"

And this morning he even left the yellow pages out on the breakfast table with a great big thick circle around "Gas Control Equipment".

He's ruddy mad is me John.

But he has me in stitches, he does.

I think that's the main reason I must have married him, 'cos he makes me laugh so much. Yer gotta laugh ain't you, or you're dead.

That's what I thinks, anyway.

And what about all them burps then? Well, I can stop them for a bit but then I has ter let them all go like they been waiting in a queue. I ain't really bothered like, 'cos I feels good and I reckon I been holding all this stuff in for too ruddy long, I have.

And I been thinking about all these memories and as how they're all connected, like. I mean they're all about me not saying anything, aren't they? And about me family not noticing me - and me not saying nothing to them, neither.

Like I were holding me breath and biting me tongue all at the same time. And it ain't no wonder me body became all puffed up tight; like a puffer fish.

And now I just feels, well... *loose*.

You know?

So when I rings up his lordship I tells him about most of this burping and farting. Not the bit about me and John obviously.

'Cos that bit's private, ain't it?

I did tell him that by the time I got home, I was that tired I fell asleep just sitting up in the arm chair; and I never does that. And I told him as how, after that sleep, for the next three nights I hardly slept at all, did I?

Less than 2 hours a night I reckon, but I had so much energy in the day time it were like I was wired up to the national grid, you know?

And I tells him as how I feels ruddy wonderful. Lighter and all renewed, like. And as how me mates keep saying,

"What the ruddy hell are you on, Mavis Brown?"

And I told him as how I keep smiling all the time and they keep saying,

"What's so ruddy funny - are you taking the piss?"

'Course I didn't tell him how - driving home after that session - as well as farting and burping for England, I couldn't stop me mind racing through all me life like a film, you know, going real fast with all the happy stuff and all the sad stuff as well. Nor as how there were this ache in me chest and I were crying and feeling happy, all at the same time.

Don't get me wrong, I could have told him and I know he would have listened but I just didn't want to, did I? I suppose I didn't need to, really.

'Cos I had me John didn't I?

Chapter forty-four

Nor did I tell his lordship that when me John got home that night, I only burst into tears like a daft ruddy cow, didn't I?

Nor as how I couldn't stop talking that evening to me John - sitting at the dining room table - about all me childhood memories. Nor as how he just listened and held me hand and all these words kept pouring outta me like I had ruddy verbal diarrhoea, you know? But I just knew he was taking me seriously and like he understood that this was really important for me to put it all together like, and to speak like this.

And sometimes I cried, didn't I?

'Cos there was just this great sadness for so much that never happened in me life or were just never said and sometimes even he had tears in his eyes.

Which was even worse, weren't it?

And I kept talking about the past and then the present and what I wanted for the future and how me body must have been so frozen all these years and me not saying nothing to nobody about falling off that bus and nearly dying, even!

And if me own girls had to keep quiet about summat important like that I would be so upset, wouldn't I? And how terrible I feels that I never told nobody about that pervert on the bike and nobody reporting him to the police, like.

And how many little girls did he go on and mess with; all 'cos I never said nothing? And that really made me cry to think of all them poor frightened little girls...

And me whole ruddy-stupid-thick-family just not knowing how to deal with me getting into college and then me doing so well and them not even knowing it deserved celebrating, like.

Me knowing nothing about living, basically.

Except wanting to make our John's babies and make them all a nice home. And all the way through he said nothing did he, the ruddy saint? He just kept holding me hand and looking in me eyes like he could listen to me forever.

And all that's just too private to tell his lordship, ain't it?

Nor did I never tell him how me John came home one night, a couple of months later on, and said we was going out to eat for a change and to put on summat nice, like. And so we wheels our Mickey out - he gets all excited when we goes out - and walks to our favourite Greek restaurant around the corner and I almost dies 'cos there in the restaurant is me girls and all our mates and there's this ruddy great banner across the wall that says "Graduation 1978 - Congratulations Mavis!"

And everyone's cheering and clapping and me John stands up, and says that some things is just too important to forget to celebrate, even if it's thirty years late! And I'm just blubbering and sniffing like a whale with a cold, aren't I?

And then at the end of the meal that mad Greek bugger, Davros - you know, him what owns the restaurant - wheels in a trolley full of plates and gives them out and suddenly everyone's looking at me.

And I don't do stuff like that, do I?

Well not before, like.

I mean I used to watch all them mad Greeks do the plate smashing thing. But I never joined in, did I?

Only I'm different now, ain't I?

So I lifts me arm holding the plate high up in the air and they're all looking at me and saying stuff like "Go on, Mavis!" and I looks at all me mates, smiling at me like, with their eyes all sparkling and bright and their happy faces and I thinks what a ruddy great life I've had. And I thinks as how this is what it all comes down to, don't it? I mean no matter what yer past is, there's always right now.

And just because I haven't done stuff before ain't no reason to stop meself doing it now. I mean what are we, friggin' robots what is programmed?

Not me, mate.

Not Mavis Brown.

So I looks at all me friends and I wanna hold this moment forever, I do. 'Cos this is me crossin' the friggin' Rubicon, it is.

This is me right now.

Choosing what I do, no matter what happened in the past.

And then I brings that plate right down and lets it go smashing onto the stone floor and suddenly we're all shouting and smashing them plates and cheering and I feels like them plates is me past and the way I locked everything into me body. And smashing them plates on the floor into little bits is the cleanest sound I ever heard before or since, it is.

All cleansing, like

Chapter forty-five

And you know what else?

Nor did I tell him as how I even started dancing. For real, like. Not classes, but in front of real audiences.

See, when I were driving back down that M62 after me sessions with his lah-dee-dah-ship in Halifax, I used to love listening to that Pachelbel's Canon. You know, the one what they played in *Love Story*. Me John and I love that film, we do.

Soft buggers that we are.

Anyway, I was driving home after one session and I just kept thinking as how I could actually feel his lordship doing different strokes on different parts of me body as I listened to that music, like. And then I begins to see the whole thing like a dance.

So I starts to choreograph it in me head - just for a laugh, really - thinking as how nice it would be to see a Massage that were like a dance, you know?

With music.

Anyways I was visiting me old Aromatherapy college - 'cos they asked me back to teach some strokes, like - and I were telling one of the students about it during the break and she only goes and tells the other girls and then they all starts asking me ter show them what I meant, like.

So like a silly cow I went and put on the music, didn't I? I would never have done that before, I wouldn't.

Not the old Mavis Brown.

And I gave a Massage to one of them students exactly as how I had seen it in me head, all those times on the M62, and the rest was all watching. And when I were doing it I felt like I had come home.

I really did.

Something just happened inside of me and I weren't

Mavis Brown anymore. It were like I was just part of everything in the room: the music; the table; the students; the wall and even the air molecules all around us, and I felt free.

Completely free.

And when I stopped they was all standing there with their gobs wide open. And a couple of them even had tears down their faces.

Trouble was, the ruddy course tutor had only walked in while I were doing it, hadn't she? And I thought I were in fer a tellin' off 'cos I were meant to be showing them as how to massage the bum, like. But instead she started asking me all sorts of strange questions like, how often had I done that before and how did I come up with it, you know?

And before I knows it she's ringing me up at home, asking me if I could do it at their annual Aromatherapy conference, you know, the one where all the teachers go.

'Course I said no, didn't I?

But she just kept pesterin' me and ringing me up so finally I gave in.

So here I am now.

And I'm only walking onto a stage in a college in Regent's Park, London with three hundred and fifty friggin' Massage teachers from all around the world, watching me.

Three hundred and friggin' fifty!

So basically I'm dying, me.

I mean when I agreed to do it, I thought there might be maybe, twenty or thirty people there - 'cos I ain't never been to one of these conferences before - but not this many.

So I gets me course tutor onto the table 'cos she's agreed to be the client, hasn't she? And then I whispers to her,

"You gotta be friggin' joking, mate. I can't massage in front of all these teachers. I still don't know where half the ruddy muscles are nor what they're even called, like."

And she just says that I ain't got no choice.

And then she says the sweetest thing. She says,

"Mavis Brown, you've got more Massage knowledge in your little fingers than half of that lot of old cronies put together. Now get on with it!"

So I does.

I closes me eyes and pretends that I'm back at me old college with them nice students; the ones what I know. And the same thing happens; only this time it were worse. 'Cos this time I went flying like I did with his lordship, you know like in a friggin' helicopter!

And it were like I were wired up to an electricity station with all them people watching me and it were wild, like. And when I landed on planet Earth at the end, and opened me eyes - 'cos I'd shut me eyes tight to stop meself getting scared - well, when I stopped and opened me eyes, there was this horrible silence.

And I didn't know what to do or where to look, so I just stood there looking at me feet and then at me course tutor lying on the table on this great big stage thinking, I must be the daftest friggin' cow in the whole ruddy great Universe...

'Cos nobody liked it did they?

Obviously.

And then someone coughed.

And then I notices that several people were sniffing down in the front row. And then someone clapped. And then, well, the place just erupted.

And soon they was all standing and cheering like they had just come out of a lovely dream and they was all happy, like.

And it made me cry it did; all them people clapping and cheering.

At me,

Mavis Brown!

So now I gets asked to give this dance to all sorts of Massage conferences and schools, so I reckons I'm a real professional dancer, me. So you better watch your "p's and q's" when yer talks to me from now on, 'cos I'm right posh and you know what? Sometimes they even gives me a dressing room before I do it.

A dressing room!

And I thought I was the daft bat around here.

So I might tell his lordship one day.
Then again, I might not.
But every time I do this dance - and I've made up some more since then - I'm back on that M62, you know? Travellin' back from one of them sessions. It's like I went through me whole life on that motorway.

The best thing is, I knows I *could* tell him now. If I wanted to, like.

Before I couldn't tell nobody nothing.

What I like most about working with his lordship was that he always respected me privacy and never *pried*, like.

You know what?

Apart from me John, there weren't a single person what had noticed me and respected me like that, before.

Not one person

Chapter forty-six

So if we could just leave Mavis there, for a bit?

I want to say a little more about this whole touch thing, actually. You see, I spend so much time doing it these days - touch I mean - that I take it for granted. But some things just shouldn't be kept secret; especially when I think they might contain the missing link to all the madness in our world. Which is what I think about touch, see?

I keep meaning to write it all down in a book to let the other Massage professionals know what I do and what I've learned over these twenty years or so of touching; in case it helps them.

But I don't, do I?

No excuses, but I just stop myself and think, *hubris,* old sport. I mean tidy up your own house before giving advice to others, perhaps?

Hubris

And every time I sit down to write some *theory,* all I can actually think of are my beautiful, brave clients. All I want to do is to tell their stories.

And this Mavis is a good one, she is. But there is something else I want to share with you, if you don't mind listening, that is? Thing is, I've discovered that touch is almost as important as breathing, actually.

Certainly more important than food.

Enough research to weigh down and break several shelves in a library about this, if you're sad enough to be bothered to spend years of your life reading it.

Which I am, actually

Rather lost the plot regarding touch over here in the west we have, I'm afraid. Even worse: as the whole world becomes industrialised *everyone's losing it.*

The plot, I mean.

We do really have to be a little careful here, rather like the whole ecology thing. If we let things go too far wrong we could be in deep trouble. Know how bad it's got? Even starting to say touch is dangerous now, we are. Don't allow teachers to cuddle our crying children anymore, do we? Dads feel guilty touching their own kids in the parks, even.

Yet from animals to humans all the research says the same damn thing: lose touch and we die. 'Course we don't just walk along the street and drop down dead, do we?

We start to display all sorts of *indicators* beforehand if we stop touching, we do. So what are they then, these *indicators*?

Well, here's the list:

- *Illness*, especially immune collapse;

- *Loss of faculties*, say early onset of Alzheimer's;

- *Loss of reproductive ability* and low sperm count;

- *Withdrawal* from social groups and increasing isolation, like children playing solitary computer games;

- *Delinquency* and anti-social behaviour;

- *Irritability* and yes, violence.

Loss of *caring*, actually.

All from not having touch, see?

All the research says it over and over again; I could quote it, chapter and verse. But it all just comes down to this: we are simply not reaching out and touching each other enough, anymore.

So we start to see these *indicators* appearing all over the place, don't we? Anyone seen these signs popping up around the place, perhaps? Because that's what happens first, see.

Indicators

Then we drop down dead from the cancers and sickness,

as well as all the violence from each other. Getting out of touch with each other, we are.

People not caring any more.

No one stopping to let someone else through the door, anymore. Polite behaviour, see? Thinking about others around us. Looking after neighbours.

Seems to be all hurry, hurry, hurry and stress. All silly, selfish aggression and road rage, actually. Shame really, because we human beings can be so noble and so damned magnificent, when we want to be.

You know what?

Societies that have maintained touch from birth show a different picture entirely, they do. Health and harmony, actually. Distinct lack of any criminal elements at all.

Social cohesion.

Community.

Lots of smiles and happiness, not to put too fine a point on it. When babies are born, know what they do? Wrap them in papooses and walk about with them *attached*. Keep skin on skin contact for almost a year. Forget about those nappies - just learn when your baby is going to do a whoopsie and take measures! Don't wrap them up in clothing, keep 'em close to Mater's body for suckling.

Mmmm...

Yummy yum yum

But breast feeding isn't just about food, see?

It's about the hands and the lips, actually: the two parts of the body with the richest supply of nerves. There are more touch receptor nerves around the mouth and the hands, than in the rest of the body put together. Only one of the many obvious things missed by our jolly clever *modern* medicine.

Of course the brain needs the stimulation of touch so we can grow, but we really need it so we feel *soothed*. We humans need a lot of *soothing* we do.

Though we don't always like to admit it.

So reach out and touch someone today, why don't you, eh? Give them a handshake. Give them a hug, if they want one. Stroke a pet. Touch someone's face, stroke their hair, put your arm around them, old sport.

It's natural, see?

Don't listen to the social workers, okay? Ignore the bureaucrats. Don't let them think they can run the world, please.

And listen, here's another thing:

The more you touch another person, the healthier and happier *you* get.

The hands, see?

Nerve rich, they are. The more you give, the more you receive. Big house rule, that one.

So give someone's back a rub or massage their hands or feet with some cream, for a treat. Make them lie down and close their eyes while you do it. Put on some nice music. Don't worry about whether you are doing it right or wrong. Just trust your instincts.

Natural, see?

Let them drift away to the land of nod. And see how you feel after. Give it a go. 'Course *they* will love it, if they let go. But how do *you* feel?

You will feel good as well.

I guarantee it.

Only one more thing to add:

Today is national "Touch another human being day". Every day is, actually. So reach out and touch someone, okay?

Thanks for listening

Chapter forty-seven

Now when I says me Mam and me Dad was ruddy daft, I don't mean nothing by it, don't get me wrong.

'Cos I'm a Mam meself and I think it's important to just say here, that I thinks me Mam and me Dad were good people and they never wished any harm on me at all, they didn't.

They was just ignorant, weren't they?

And what the hell was they supposed to do with this ugly little duckling what was always asking these uncomfortable ruddy *scientific* questions - I loved science, I did - and they just couldn't know who I was, or where I was coming from.

'Cos they were pretty messed up themselves, weren't they? And that weren't none of their fault neither, just like what happened to me weren't none of my fault.

I mean the way me Mam learned that her Dad had died, is just awful. He worked down the Albert docks and operated a crane, didn't he? And his crane unbalanced and he crashed 200 feet to his death. And she learned about this when a copper come to our street and knocked on the door, and she were only eleven and she said as how her Mam and Dad was both out at work, and all this ruddy copper said was,

"Well your dad ain't never coming back 'cos he's dead, girl" and then he walked off down the street. And she ain't never really got over that 'cos she loved her Dad with all her heart, she did. And just before she died last month, she says to me,

"I really misses me Daddy, pet."

And her eighty-nine years old an' all.

So they both had their own problems like the rest of us,

didn't they? And they could never understand me. Well they never really knew me, did they? 'Cos from the age of two I never said much at all, after that bucket in the kitchen.

And now I knows why.

I reckon I just froze up, I did.

So how the hell could they know me after that? And from the age of ten, I think I always knew I didn't fit in with me family. I used to spend ages going through me Mam and me Dad's old papers in the dining room, every Saturday afternoon when they went out to the footie match. I were that certain I would find me adoption certificate - honest! I was just certain I would find it in there, somewhere.

I think I actually *wanted* to find out I were adopted, 'cos then it would explain why me family always felt so ruddy *alien* to me. And then as I grew up, I never really had any friends, did I?

Little Billy-no-mates, me!

I mean, it's hard to have mates when you don't hardly say nothing at all, except chunnerin' away inside your head like, ain't it? And when I was a kid, I never invited me friends round, and me Mam never talked to the other kids' parents like I saw all the other mums doing, after school.

All I can really remember, is getting me own tea and me Mam working till late, always doing for someone else and always being worried about money. So I were alone really; until I met me John, of course.

I don't know why John were so patient with me, I really don't but it's like his love for me saved me ruddy life, didn't it?

And I knows I could never earn that much love, even if I worked for it every minute of me life, you know? And I think that's why I didn't want to teach after I qualified as a teacher, 'cos all I wanted was to have me John's kids and bring them up, and I think they taught me what love is all about; 'cos I learned everything I know from those kids, I did.

I learned how to laugh and to cry and have fun, and I think I sort of did it all for meself really, you know, selfish like. 'Cos I knew I just had to be close and watch and learn from them. 'Cos I was never really allowed to be a littl'un meself, were I? What with me Mam out all the time, and her always so sad and bitter?

And when we adopted our Mickey - he were only seven, then - well, he was the biggest teacher of them all; 'cos he really couldn't speak, could he? So I had to learn as how to speak for him, didn't I? And it was like finding not just me own voice, but having to use me voice to fight fer our Mickey with all them doctors and ruddy social workers, what thinks they knows best.

But he just lets me know with his eyes, he does and I has to tell 'em what for, which is why I won't ever let anyone else do for our Mickey, not as long as I have breath in me lungs, I won't.

And who would believe that after all this Massage, and after his ruddy lordship has done his magic on me, I would go and spend the rest of me friggin' time going around teaching people how to touch and Massage each other?

That's the same Mavis Brown what vowed she would never ruddy teach nobody not never again after her first year in school, 'cos all she really wanted was to stay at home with her family where she were safe; and all the sunshine seemed to come out from inside the house, didn't it?

But the Massage changed all that. Now look at me - I can't ruddy well shut up, can I? Nor does I want to. I mean, you can't just hide away when you don't like what's going on, can you? You have to face it and deal with it.

'Course I had realised some of this stuff about me life - over the years with our John I had realised I didn't have to live me life the way me family had - that it was mostly a load of old rubbish what they said and believed, you know? And that living life their way wouldn't never help nobody, would it?

And I knew I could choose me own family and John and I could do things just as how we like, and we likes what we do a lot, don't we?

But what I really learned from all this, is that growing up in me family was like having someone plug a video cassette into me brain and then it keeps playing and playing and playing no matter how crap the video or how often I keeps pressing the stop button - it just keeps playing.

But over me years with John and me kids, I learned to take them videos outta me head - hundreds of them. But what I hadn't realised 'til now was this:

I were putting them in me body, instead.

'Cos now I were with our John and me kids and doing a lotta nice stuff, me head were filled with my new life, you know? So there weren't no space for them old family videos in me head. So I carried them round in me body instead, like; in me arms and me legs an in me ruddy shoulders. And the healthier me life become and the more me mind become free of me family's stupid ways of living, the more them videos were leaving me head, weren't they?

But they was all going straight into me body.

And now I realises that what his lordship's Massage did, was to let them videos come out of me body.

Don't get me wrong, 'cos it's not like I wants to get rid of them for good, is it?

'Cos them videos is me life.

They's what makes me who I am today, and I will always love me Mam and our Dad for making me who I am. I think the saddest thing on the planet - apart from social workers, that is - is those people what goes around the place moaning about their parents and blaming them for everything that's gone wrong in their lives.

And them all fully grown up, and some even parents themselves!

So I doesn't want to throw them videos away, do I? I just wants to put them in some library round the corner like, so I can visit and play them again whenever I wants. And now me body can be loose and soft and free again, which it ain't really been since I were two.

Sometimes I just wanna run me finger along them videos, see? Not even play them like, but I likes to remember the different videos, and as how they helped me get to being here. 'Cos I likes who I am and I likes me life, I do.

Really.

I feels so lucky.

Them videos don't mess up me head or me body these days, do they? They don't weigh me down, neither. The Massage has helped me to find a new sense of freedom inside meself. 'Course I can't be sure of anything in the future, can I? I mean, who can?

But I knows one thing; I wants to continue this journey of discovering and releasing stuff out of my body.

'Cos there's stuff in all of us that like, binds us to the ground

Chapter forty-eight

Me secret dream is to fly - I mean really fly.

Not in a plane or nothing, but just to lift off and fly. 'Cos I thinks that when we takes all this heavy bad stuff out of the body - when it's all completely gone - then I think we changes and we becomes something else. I know this sounds ruddy crackers like, but I do believe we can do anything we wants to.

Anything.

And I knows that I just wants ter fly like a bird, I do. And now I knows that this journey ain't over, not by a long shot; I still have tension that I can release and I can become as free as I want to be.

And one day I will really fly.

That's what I believes, anyway.

You can call me crackers if yer want

Chapter forty-nine

So here I am, Mavis Brown, standing outside me front door looking up at the beautiful sky and listening to all them birds, and guess what I'm holding in me hand?

'Cos you wanna know what me and John just did?

We gave our house a name, didn't we? I didn't see why I should just be another ruddy number, I didn't; I mean, I ain't lived me whole friggin' life just to be a number, have I?

And John, bless him, got all excited about it and he's put a nice slate plaque on the front wall with the new name on it. And we told all our friends and asked them to send us letters with the new address on - well, they all knows we're crazy anyway - and I'm holding them letters now in me hand.

And from now on, everytime a letter arrives it says this house name on the front, like it's a message from God.

And you know what?

I think everyone should do this 'cos it's ruddy marvellous; and just think of all the chaos it would cause all them mail order companies if you got rid of yer house number and just put a name on, instead!

No more junk mail.

So today is national "Give your house a special name" day.

I mean, think as how the poor ruddy postmen will be scratching their heads with all these ruddy names, trying to work out what Mrs Poops has called her house, this week!

Nobody should just be a number, should they? I mean posh people does it - has all them houses with names on them - so why shouldn't the rest of us?

So our house ain't number twelve anymore, is it? Our

house has a name, it does. The name of our house is now:
'Carpe Diem'.

Seize the day.
And that's just what I'm gonna do. And I hopes you does, too.

Good luck to yer, mate

About the Author

Gerry Pyves was born in New Zealand in 1957 and then grew up in the UK. In 1982, after being a school teacher for several years, he changed careers to the world of Complementary Medicine and Massage therapy. He had a successful Massage clinic in Swiss Cottage, London and then moved north to Hebden Bridge, where he now lives with his family.

He has been doing Massage for over twenty-five years and is well known in the profession for his approach and publications.

In 1997, he also qualified in Transactional Analysis Psychotherapy and as a UKCP registered psychotherapist.

Gerry now divides his working time between his Massage clinic, his international Massage training company and writing.

This is his first novel.

More From Shi'Zen Publications

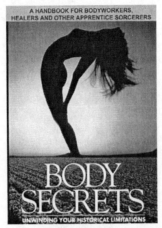

Body Secrets
Unwinding Your Historical Limitations
by Don McFarland

This bodywork classic has long been out of print. Shi'Zen has re-printed this book for the benefit of all who are interested in healing and personal development.

If you let it, the body will tell you its secrets.
And having told them, will be free to move on.
This is a book about listening to those secrets.

The author, Don McFarland, is one of the world's leading authorities on the power of touch to transform our lives. A must read for anyone who is seeking to understand more about the secrets that lie within our bodies and how to touch others.

Shi'Zen Publications
PO Box 57, Hebden Bridge, West Yorkshire, HX7 6WW
+44 (0) 1422 843 842